Succes

CW00687138

Moving to

Spain

A step-by-step Guide to Immigration, Becoming a Resident, and Happily Living in Spain from outside of the EU

Vicki Franz

ISBN: 9798815827622

23 22

PARA MI FAMILIA

For my parents Henning and Kirsten, and my sister Undine, who have supported me from the beginning of my life in Spain and always have an open door for us when homesickness overcomes me.

Y para mis suegros, Mercedes y Eduard, y para mi tía española Ana. Por acogerme con los brazos abiertos y hacerme sentir una más en la familia.

And of course, for my husband Eduardo, my partner in the paper war of the Spanish red tape and my struggle with Catalan grammar. Thank you for never giving up. T'estimo.

Table of contents

Moving to Spain – to live where others go on vacation. Experiencing the relaxed atmosphere under the Spanish sun while enjoying life to the fullest. For many, this is a long-held dream. But for most, it remains just that – a dream. However, once you have taken this step and successfully built a life in Spain, you usually fall completely for this beautiful country.

So what is the difference between these kinds of emigrants, who after only a short time in Spain have to return home penniless and desolate, and those who call their move to Spain the best decision of their lives? Proper preparation makes all the difference.

By purchasing this book, you are already a decisive step ahead of many dreamers out there. What you hold in your hands is the first step into an exciting new phase of your life that you will never forget – the beginning of your personal adventure in Spain. In the following pages, I will take you by the hand and step-by-step help you turn your dream of Spain into reality. Whether it's a year abroad, a long-term vacation, studies, a language course, work, retirement, or a meaningful new start in sunny Spain, in this complete package, you'll find not only detailed step-by-step instructions that will make your move to Spain fundamentally easier but also lots of valuable tips from already experienced expats. I'll tell you what documents you need to live and work in Spain, and where exactly you can get them. With these practical instructions, I want to save you dozens of hours of annoying research, through which I had to torture myself after my own arrival in the country. In addition, I'll give you helpful first words and phrases that are guaranteed to pay off when you register in the country. I want to help you socialize and settle into the country as soon as you arrive. With this book, I want to show you how to go from being a guest in the country to becoming a fully-fledged resident of Spain and getting the most out of your new phase of life. Throughout the following few chapters, you'll find out what else is behind living in Spain besides paella and Julio Iglesias.

But maybe you're still unsure about whether Spain is really the right place for you. Because, let's face it, not everyone is made for a life in Spain. But don't worry, even in this case, this book can serve as a practical decision-making aid and prevent you from making a hasty decision. Even if you decide not to move to Spain after reading this book, at least this guide will have saved you from a few stress wrinkles and a big disappointment.

What makes a good expat

"Whoever wants to travel must first bring love for the country and its people, at least no bias. He must have good will to find the good instead of killing it by critical comparisons." – Theodor Fontane

You can apply this quote from the famous German writer Theodor Fontane not only to traveling but also to staying in another country in general. The ideal immigrant should therefore be open-minded towards a different culture and the inhabitants. This is the only way you will be able to fully immerse yourself in your new life in Spain. In a tourism lecture, my professor once said mutatis mutandis: "Many vacationers are only looking to vacation in their own country, but abroad." Because let's face it, who doesn't know this guy? — That James Smith who flies to Ibiza and gets burned crab-red just to stay on a diet of burgers and fries exclusively, and depends on everyone around him to speak English? While that may be understandable for a vacation, as an expat, you might want to approach your move with a more open mind. You should aim to learn about the culture of your adopted country, try new things, and get involved in local life.

In addition, good preparation is essential when emigrating. Although chance and the whim of the official who issues your documents on the spot also play a particular role in the process, you can avoid many time wasters and faux pas with correct planning. However, try not to get lost in detail either. Because one lesson you can't learn early enough for your move to Spain is: things never go as planned anyway. So get used to the *Qué será, será* attitude of the Spaniards already, and let's find a reasonable middle way together to make your time in Spain a complete success.

Ideally, you as an emigrant also have a lot of patience for long waits at government offices in your luggage. If this is not the case, crossword puzzles or other pastimes will do the trick.

Reasons for moving to Spain

There can be many reasons to emigrate to Spain - the good weather, the delicious food, the Mediterranean Sea, or the Spaniards' relaxed attitude to life. Spain simply exerts a magical attraction on us Westerners and lures almost 84 million tourists to the country every year. It's hardly surprising that many of us don't want to miss that typical *Spain feeling*. Maybe you have personal reasons and want to move to Spain because of love or work. In the following section, I would like to show you some fantastic advantages and reasons for living in Spain[1].

The weather – Spain offers almost 300 days of sunshine a year, depending on the region. The daily dose of sun not only tans your skin but also lifts your spirits. Say goodbye to the long gray, depressing winters of your home country because in Spain, the winters are short, sunny, and mild from the ground up.

A relaxed lifestyle – Spaniards are famous for their laid-back approach to life, a siesta here, a sip of vino there, and their "*everything will work out somehow*" attitude. The weather makes it possible to spend a lot of time outside in the fresh air, sitting with friends and especially *familia* after eating together and talking about everything under the sun.

Mediterranean delicacies – Another essential factor that speaks for living in Spain is its unique cuisine. Traditional family recipes meet fresh ingredients to create the most amazing dishes. This makes Spanish cuisine one of the most popular and healthiest in the world. It is not for nothing that Spain is currently considered the healthiest country in the world.

An outstanding healthcare system – If you are living in Spain as a long-term resident (you can apply for long-term residency after five years of continuously living in the country) or on a work visa, you have access to one of the best healthcare systems in the world, completely free of charge. The hospitals in the country are equipped with the latest technology and competent professionals.

Fascinating landscapes – Spain is full of unique natural landscapes and simply has a little bit of everything to offer. You can find white sandy beaches and turquoise waters, unique cities with historic architecture, Mediterranean pine forests and waterfalls, scenic mountain landscapes, and even ski resorts in this diverse country.

The language – Spanish is not only considered one of the most learned but also one of the most important and most spoken languages in the world. So a move or stay is a great way to familiarize yourself with the language or deepen your language skills. For those who like something a little more out of the ordinary, some of the country's provinces also offer the chance to give Spain's second official languages a try, such as Catalan.

Life is more affordable – On average, it is estimated that life in Spain is up to 45 % cheaper than in the UK and US. So if you want to take a year off or enjoy your well-deserved retirement, you simply get more out of your money here. As always, however, it all depends on where exactly you live, where you used to live (the cost of living in the various provinces varies significantly in some cases - more on that later) and what your lifestyle and thus your expenses look like.

International experience for your CV – Professional experience abroad looks great on your resume and may even be a decision criterion by some employers. Such experiences abroad can be, for example, studies, semesters abroad, internships, volunteer work, regular work, or a language course.

Simply a great time – Whatever your reasons for moving to Spain may be, and no matter how much time you plan to spend in the country, one thing is certain - your life abroad will simply be a unique experience that you will remember for a lifetime.

Always a connection home – Living in Spain is a dream, but when homesickness strikes, one of the many daily flight connections can take you back to the UK or the US in a flash and at a reasonable price for a visit home.

You are not alone – It is estimated that in 2019, there were about 5.5 million immigrants living in Spain. So it's not that hard to meet other emigrants and find connections. Even if you are not looking for other expats but only want to get in touch with locals, you can benefit from the experiences and tips of other emigrants, for example, with this book.

Outgrowing yourself – Living (alone) in Spain is not always easy, and every beginning is hard. Abroad, you will be confronted with a new everyday life, different cultures, a new language, and situations outside your comfort zone. But this is exactly what can help you grow beyond yourself and strengthen your self-confidence.

Love – For many immigrants, love is the main reason for moving to Spain. At the time, I also moved to

Barcelona mainly for my husband, Eduardo. As you see, such an international relationship can undoubtedly have a future. It is truly a wonderful feeling to finally be able to live together after months of a long-distance relationship.

Reasons against moving to Spain

As beautiful as life in Spain can be, and without sugarcoating things, you should be aware that starting over in another country is not always a walk in the park. Spain, like any place, comes with its advantages and disadvantages, which means, conversely, that life in this country does not come with peace and joy for everyone. Ideally, you will have already experienced the Spanish mentality and attitude to life on one trip or another before you take the big step of emigrating. In the following section, you will find a few points that could speak against a possible future in Spain.

Career options – If you're looking for a well-paying job with all its security and opportunities for advancement, you'll need either a lot of luck, excellent language skills, or good contacts in Spain. With an unemployment rate of 13 % (as of December 2022) and a youth unemployment rate of around 30 %, there are, unfortunately, very few good career opportunities in the country. For immigrants in particular, searching for work in specific career fields therefore often proves unsuccessful.

Lower salary – If you do find a job, you should be aware that wages in Spain, in general, are lower than in the UK and the US. While the average US salary is about € 60 k and the UK salary € 37.6 k per year, the average Spaniard earns only € 25 k per year. Although the cost of living in the country is correspondingly lower, you should expect very high rental prices in certain cities in Spain, such as Madrid and Barcelona.

Spanish red tape – Every single expat will probably tell you the same: The official procedures in Spain are perhaps by far the most significant disadvantage of living in Spain. For every little process, you need 500 different documents and another one because it's Tuesday. The highlight of going through authorities is when documents are required that don't even exist (I wish I were joking). But don't worry, this book is designed to keep your new gray hairs that come with moving to Spain in check and at least give you a rough idea of all the government processes.

Safety – The safety in Spain itself is estimated to be generally slightly higher than in the US and UK. Since family life in Spain sometimes takes place deep into the night, you can often still walk through the streets in the dark without hesitation. However, some laws make corruption in various areas or even pickpockets in the country an easy game - over the course of the book, you will learn more about this topic.

Security –When you look at legal and financial security, you can see apparent differences between the countries. For one thing, the concept of unemployment benefits can differ greatly between Spain and other countries. But also, the security in your life plays a role. Emigrating to another country and building an entirely new life always involves a certain amount of risk. To get a foothold in Spain, you first must break out of your usual framework and leave your comfort zone.

International cuisine – Spanish food is excellent, and a dream come true for many. In big cities and tourist areas, you can also find plenty of international restaurants. However, if you like to cook international food yourself at home, you will quickly notice that Spanish supermarkets mainly focus on national food.

Although more and more international products have been on offer in recent years, these are usually only available in specialty stores or are relatively expensive.

Language barrier – How little did I know when I moved to Spain with my B1-Spanish certificate and actually believed I'd be able to communicate with natives in no time. But let me tell you, speaking Spanish on paper is quite different from having real conversations with locals. Depending on how much exposure you have to the language and your level of basic Spanish, it will most certainly take you several months to really be able to engage in conversations with locals. It usually takes several years to reach a native or completely fluent level. In addition, there are regional differences, strong dialects in certain parts of the country, slang, and second official languages in some provinces, such as Catalan and Basque. And even if you eventually become fluent in the language, you will still be mistaken for a tourist by many locals just because of your accent or appearance.

Temperatures – If you're a true summer child like me, you can count this point among the positives of living in Spain. For many, however, the country's temperatures are a major complaint. Depending on the region, temperatures regularly reach around 40° C/ 104° F in the summer. Winters tend to be milder, but poorly equipped homes, lack of heating, and unsealed windows make for a cold winter in some areas.

Cultural barrier – Spain is a country incredibly rich in culture, customs, and traditions. And for the first few years, it's fascinating to spend the various holidays in the country and experience them together with locals. However, those who stay in Spain permanently will have to come to terms with the fact that some of their own traditions, which they followed for years before moving, do not exist in Spain in the same way. Such traditions may include Christmas traditions, Thanksgiving, 4th July, snow (usually snow falls in very few areas of Spain), or looking each other in the eye while toasting (that one is a typical tradition from Germany).

Mañana, Mañana – Even though some perceive the *mañana-mentality* of the Spanish as an advantage, it is a constant thorn in the side of many expats. The attitude that things can still be done tomorrow (*mañana*) means that many processes proceed much more slowly than necessary. Not only official procedures but also personal events thus sometimes seem to drag on indefinitely. I, as a German, simply lack the pinch of patience required for this attitude. The Spanish *mañana attitude*, if you will, is thus probably the most prominent cultural difference between Spain and many other Western countries.

Homesickness – One factor that is often disregarded in the decision about moving abroad is homesickness. Those who move to another country usually leave friends and family behind in their home country. And even if Spain is only a flight away from your country of origin, it is still impossible for most of us to fly home for every family celebration or important event with our friends. So before you make your decision, be aware that from now on, you will miss some events back home and won't be able to see your loved ones as often as before.

Dreams and reality – While on vacation in Spain, every day is special. Long walks on the beach under the Spanish sun, paella, as many tapas as you can eat, and happy faces everywhere you look. However, anyone living in Spain knows that it's easy to fall into a regular daily routine here. Very few people spend every day at the beach, and even the delicious tapas aren't quite as special when you can eat them every day. You should therefore be prepared for the fact that the vacation feeling will eventually fade, and daily routine will take over. How you organize your everyday life in the country, however, is of course entirely up to you.

Comparison between life in Spain, the US, and the UK

	Spain	USA	UK
Temper atures	The average temperature is between 17.1° and 18.8°C[2] (63°F and 65.84°F)	The average temperature is around 12°C (54.5°F)	The average temperature is between 6°C and 14°C (43°F and 56°F)
Weather	Estimated average of 60 rainy days per year	Estimated average of 110 rainy days per year[3]	Estimated average of 133 rainy days per year
Prices	Approx. 30 to 40 % cheaper than the US and 17 to 25 % cheaper than the UK	Approx. 40 to 60 % more expensive than Spain	Approx. 20 to 30 % more expensive than Spain

	Spain	**USA**	**UK**
Job Market	More than 13 % of the country is unemployed. It can therefore often be difficult to find a good job[4]	Depending on location promising career opportunities; the unemployment rate is 3.4 %[5]	Depending on location good career opportunities; the unemployment rate is 3.7 %[6]
Average Income	ca. € 25,104	ca. € 59,973[7]	ca. € 37,609
Bureau-cracy	Usually very chaotic	It depends on the state you are in, but usually quite structured	Can be quite confusing due to Brexit but generally structured
Health	Spain ranks #1 in Bloomberg's Healthiest Country Index	The US ranks 35th in Bloomberg's Healthiest Country Index	The UK ranks 19th in Bloomberg's Healthiest Country Index

	Spain	USA	UK
Happiness	Spain is ranked 29th in the World Happiness Report[8]	The USA is ranked 16th in the World Happiness Report	The UK is ranked 17th in the World Happiness Report
Corruption	35th place in international comparison (CPI 60)[9]	24th place in international comparison (CPI 69)	18th place in international comparison (CPI 73)
Internet speed	Ranked 13th in international comparison [10]	Ranked 11th in international comparison	Ranked 35th in international comparison
Number of public holidays per year	14 holidays per year	11 holidays per year	8 holidays per year

Types of stays abroad

Those who plan to move to Spain do not always have to directly intend to spend the rest of their lives in the country. There are many different ways to get to know Spain and fall in love with the country. Maybe you just want to experience living abroad temporarily. In the following section, you will find the different options that you have to spend time in Spain.

Emigrating

Let's start with the most drastic of all options. Emigrating to Spain with bag and baggage requires the most preparation time and has the most far-reaching consequences on your life. Moving to Spain means building a new life there, possibly working in the country, ideally learning the language, and adopting the customs of the country. Emigrating in particular should be well planned, and you should not rush the decision. However, once you have built a life in Spain, you rarely regret it.

Semester abroad

For students who just want to "get a taste" of the country or simply experience an unforgettable semester, a semester abroad is a great way to get to know the country. Long party nights, fun excursions, and international friendships await you. However, the catch with semesters abroad is that most students come into contact with mostly other international students, less so with locals, and thus experience Spain more from a tourist perspective. For many, however, a semester abroad is enough to make them fall madly in love with the country and its people and ultimately emigrate to Spain after their studies are over.

Internship or language school

Like a semester abroad, internships and language courses are ideal ways to gain an exciting insight into the Spanish way of life. In addition to gaining valuable work experience, internships are a great chance to expand and deepen your language skills. If you are primarily concerned with the language, an in-country language course is probably right for you. However, when choosing where to take your language course, be aware that different dialects are spoken in Spain. In general, there is probably no better way to learn a language than in the country itself. You can try out the theory you learn in class directly in real life after school. However, similar to a semester abroad, many language students generally come into contact with other international visitors they meet at the language school rather than making friends with locals.

Au-Pair

If you like to spend time with children and ideally already have some experience with childcare, you have the opportunity to go to Spain for a few months as an au pair. As an au pair you live in a family as a member, take care of the children, and help with the household. Often you have a lot of free time to explore the country and attend a language course in addition to your work as an au pair (usually you work a maximum of 30 hours a week). Most of the time, an agency brings the local families and au pairs together. The agency also takes care of your well-being on-site. Nowadays, there is also the option to get to know potential au pair families via Facebook or other portals. Working as an au pair can be a wonderful option for those going abroad alone for the first time. Living with a family and the additional language course also gives au pairs a unique opportunity to learn Spanish.

Sabbatical

A year abroad can have many faces. Maybe you just want to use your time off before starting your professional life or studies - or perhaps you just need a break from your job. During a year abroad, you can take courses, learn the language, or just enjoy life under the Spanish sun. Maybe you want to find out if life in Spain is suitable for you before moving there with all your possessions. What you do with your year is therefore entirely up to you. However, a year abroad is also possible for all location independent or digital nomads. Of course, you can also determine the exact duration of your stay yourself. Maybe your personal "year abroad" will only last a few weeks or months, or maybe it will be two years.

Professional time abroad

Perhaps the decision to go to Spain was not entirely your own idea. Many people move to Spain for professional reasons. Maybe you have been transferred or oversee a project or a particular customer on-site. Whether you are being transferred to Spain on a temporary or long-term basis or working with Spaniards or people from your own country, this should not stop you from killing two birds with one stone and taking full advantage of your time in Spain. Make sure you have enough free time on-site to get to know the country and its people and to fully enjoy

Spanish life outside of work.

Retirement

Who doesn't secretly dream of spending their retirement on the beach under palm trees? So it's hardly surprising that so many retirees are drawn to Spain after their work in their home country is done. The coasts of the mainland in particular, as well as the Spanish islands, are popular emigration destinations for people who want to spend their retirement in Spain. Due to valid tax treaties between Spain and several other countries, it is often possible to get your total pension amount paid out without any problems, even if you settle in Spain. Depending on which country you are from, you might have to pay taxes in your country for the pension you receive, e.g., as a US citizen. Your pension insurance or a tax advisor can probably advise you best on this subject.

Wintering

If you don't want to give up your residence completely, but still want to take advantage of the short, mild winter under the Spanish sun, you also have the option of spending the winter in Spain. The Canary Islands are particularly popular for this, as it is still toasty warm there, even during the winter months. Those who would like to spend a few months in Spain during the winter should either already be retired or pursue a job that can be done from either country. Such a job could be either a location-independent job or a seasonal job. Where and how exactly you become taxable, in this case, depends mainly on exactly how long you stay in the country and where you do what kind of work. To be on the safe side, it is best to consult a tax advisor on the subject. Especially in Spain, several tax advisors and lawyers specialize in international tax law. The easiest way to find contacts in your area is via Google or expat forums.

What does it cost to move to Spain?

Unfortunately, it is not possible to make a general statement about the costs you will incur when you move to Spain. This is because the exact costs depend on various factors. It already begins with whether you emigrate completely or come to the country only temporarily. It also depends on how many of your belongings must be transported to Spain. A transportation agency will certainly have to be hired if you decide to bring beloved pieces of furniture with you to your new home. On the other hand, if you are only traveling with a couple of suitcases, you have already saved money. Likewise, the total cost can increase if your belongings have to travel a further distance. A move from Munich, Germany, to Barcelona is undoubtedly cheaper than the route from Austin, Texas, to Seville. It is especially costly if your new home is on one of the Spanish islands. Because in this case, your luggage has to be transported to the respective island by container ship. In order to get a more precise idea of the delivery costs, you can contact a few shipping companies without obligation and find out about an approximate price budget.

Another cost factor is the visa fee. While the fee itself is usually not very expensive, keep in mind that it will be a repeating expense due every time you renew your visa for yourself and each dependent.

Maybe you have a car that you want to register after your move. Depending on the model and age of your vehicle, you could easily add another € 1,000 to your moving costs. You will find more information on this topic in a later chapter. The next cost item are fees for the application and translation of essential documents. There is a big difference in your expenses depending on whether you hire a Gestoría to help you or not.

Another important cost factor is the region you have chosen to live within Spain. Rent, transportation, and similar things cost different amounts in the different provinces of the country.

In order to create a moving budget and get a more accurate overview of the upcoming costs, you should add up your personal expenses of the following aspects:

- Visa costs
- Costs of private health insurance
- Potential taxes
- Costs of transporting your belongings (e.g., freight forwarding or extra luggage on the plane)
- Transportation costs (e.g., airline tickets or fuel)
- Costs for accommodation on-site (accommodation costs on arrival, brokerage costs, security payments when signing a rental contract etc.)
- Furnishing costs (new furniture, renovation work, etc.)
- Administrative costs for local documents (e.g., visa, NIE, translations of various documents, and recognition of your professional training and degrees)
- Costs for registration of your car

However, once your local registration is done and

you've found a longer-term place to live, your payments will start to smooth out. Depending on where exactly you live and what lifestyle you pursue, moving to Spain can actually pay off in the long run. This is because more often than not the cost of living in the country is significantly lower than in the UK and the US.

Cost of living in Spain

In general, we can assume that living in Spain is up to 60 % cheaper than living in the UK or US. However, this figure should be treated with caution, since

1. The average salary in Spain is almost 58 % lower than in the US and around 32 % lower than in the UK

2. This figure is an average for the country. Prices, especially for real estate and rent, can vary widely depending on the region.

For example, the national average for a one-room rental apartment in the city center is € 749.94 per month. For comparison - following the same source, the average price for the same apartment in the USA is € 1,591.98[11] and in the UK € 1,022.70.

In the capital Madrid, however, the average price for the same apartment is already around € 1,024.11. In Murcia, on the other hand, the average price is only about € 625 for a one-room apartment in the city center. This example clearly shows how much prices can vary within the country.

The average cost of living in Spain is around € 1,500 per month, while in the US, the average John Doe spends about € 3,000 a month[12] and in the UK about € 2,000.

While the cities of San Sebastian, Barcelona, Madrid, and Palma de Mallorca are by far the most expensive cities in the country, the cities of Palencia, Melilla, and Lugo are considered the cheapest cities in Spain[13].

According to estimates, shopping in Spain is up to 50 % cheaper than in the USA or UK. But again, you shouldn't just blindly trust this figure, because it all depends on what kind of product you want to buy. Since VAT in Spain is higher than in the US and the UK (currently it is 21 %[1]), it may well be that international brands are even more expensive in Spain than in your home country.

Another cost item can be leisure activities such as hobbies, gyms, club fees, and streaming services. Depending on the activity, prices in the US or UK compared to Spain may differ significantly or only slightly. Surprisingly, you tend to pay less in Spain but not always. One example might be the average price of a gym membership. In all three countries, you can expect to pay an average of between € 33 and € 37 per month. If you're more in the mood for Netflix, you'd need to pay about € 9.50 for the basic plan and € 14.50 per month for the standard subscription in the US in 2023. In the UK, the current prices are about € 7 for the basic plan and about € 11.5 for the standard subscription. While in Spain, the basic plan costs € 7.99 per month. The Spanish Netflix standard subscription, on the other hand, is currently based at € 12.99 per month, which turns out to be a little bit cheaper than in the US and a little bit more expensive than in the UK. However, we see more significant price differences for Amazon Prime. While the price per year in the US is about € 130 and in the UK about € 105, you only pay € 49.90 per year in Spain.

---

[1] The Canary Islands are an exception, as there is no value-added tax there. On the Canary Islands, only a local tax, called the *Impuesto General Indirecto de Canarias*, is due.

Moving to Spain step-by-step

In the following part of the book, you will learn every tiny step that you should take into account when moving to Spain. In the checklist, you will find an overview of the individual steps that are important for your move, starting with preparing for your move. Later you will find detailed explanations, instructions, and practical tips for each step. The checklist is also available as a free PDF version for downloading and printing in the related links[14].

Moving to Spain checklist

3 to 6 months before moving to Spain

- o Determine the length of your stay in Spain
- o Determine place of residence
- o Obtain information on visa
- o Obtain information on insurance
- o Check pension entitlements abroad
- o Learn the language
- o Organize transport of furniture
- o Cancel rental contract
- o Cancel insurances
- o Check important documents for completeness
- o Clarify career issues
- o Prepare children for move / school search
- o Make appointment with your vet if you want to bring your pet

3 months before moving day

- o Apply for your visa
- o Clarify insurance questions on-site
- o Possibly already apply for NIE at the consulate
- o Sell items you are not taking with you
- o Organize accommodation in Spain
- o Health check/stock up on medication
- o Deregister in your country
- o Deregister your car
- o Get moving papers for your pet ready
- o Say goodbye to your loved ones

After your arrival in Spain

- o Apartment search/real estate purchase
- o Job search
- o Apply for NIE/TIE
- o (Register with social security)
- o Open a Spanish bank account
- o Empadronamiento
- o (Apply for Tarjeta Sanitaria)
- o (Possibly register for private health insurance)
- o Register children at school/kindergarten

Up to 3 months after arrival in Spain

- o Apply for Residencia (EU-passport holders)
- o Car reregistration
- o Have your driver's license changed to a Spanish one

3 to 6 months before moving to Spain

Contrary to what many people might think, emigration does not start when your feet touch Spanish soil. A few months before you leave for your new home, you should already begin to make essential preparations. These steps can be crucial to the success of your experience as an expat and save you a lot of nerve-wracking hours upon arrival in Spain. In the following sections, we will take a closer look at how to adequately plan your move.

Determine your length of stay in Spain

One of the first questions you should ask yourself if you want to emigrate to Southern Europe is the approximate duration of your stay. Because depending on how long you want to live in Spain, the more the planning process could differ. If you only want to spend a few months in the country, you do not have to worry about aspects such as transporting furniture or retirement provisions outside of your country.

If you don't want to plan precisely yet, don't worry - an approximate estimate of your length of stay in the country is sufficient. In most cases, it is enough to be aware of what kind of stay abroad (e.g., a year abroad or emigration) you would like to experience. The following questions can help you with your considerations:

- Do you want to build a life in Spain or return home at some point?
- Do you want to spend a semester/year abroad?
- Do you want to build a career in Spain?
- Do you want to live permanently in Spain or just buy a second home?
- Do you want to retire in Spain?

Decide on your new place of residency

Before you start planning your stay in Spain, you should already know where you want to go or at least have decided on a region of the country. You might already have an idea of which area you want to move to. Maybe you have already discovered your dream destination during a trip to Spain, or maybe your destination in the country depends on your work or other factors. However, if you don't have a clue which area of the country might be right for you, you are invited to try the "Which Spanish region fits me?" quiz on my website[15]. However, you should take the quiz results with a pinch of salt, as the quiz is designed mainly for entertainment purposes. Below you will find some interesting questions that may help you to make a decision. Take your time to answer the questions and decide what characteristics your dream place should have. After all, you really want to feel comfortable in the place of your choice later on.

- Do you want to live near the beach?
- In which climatic conditions do you feel most comfortable?
- Do you prefer mainland or island life?
- Do you want to move to a region where only Spanish is spoken, or is a second official language okay or even desirable for you?
- Do you mind if the locals speak a strong dialect?

- Do you prefer living in a big city, small town, or rural area?
- Would you like to move to a region where many other expatriates live?
- How important are nature and hiking opportunities in your area?

Your personal answers to these questions can give you an initial idea about which place in Spain is most or not at all suitable for you. If proximity to the beach is important to you, then all areas that are located in the interior of the country can already be omitted. This way, you can narrow down the search for your dream destination. The climate also varies greatly depending on which part of the country you choose to live in. While milder temperatures prevail on the coast, it can get sweltering in the south of the country in the summer. On the other hand, the Canary Islands have a pleasant subtropical climate all year round. The language spoken can also be an essential deciding factor. While Spanish is the primary language spoken in many regions of the country, there are some autonomous provinces where an additional official language is used. In addition, there are strong dialects, especially in the south of Spain, which could make it challenging to get started with Spanish. You will learn more about languages and dialects in a later part of this book. For some immigrants, it is also important to move to a region where there are already many or as few other expats as possible. The most popular destinations among Brits are the province of Alicante, Costa del Sol, and Costa Brava, while many Americans in particular live in the capital Madrid. The Mediterranean coast of Catalonia, Valencia and Madrid are generally popular with foreigners. But a lot of international immigrants also settle down between Andalusia, the Balearic Islands, and the Canary Islands.

Once you have decided on a region or province of the

country, you can start more thorough research. Check the internet, travel guides, and expat forums for tips and recommendations on which place, maybe even which neighborhood, might be right for you. For all emigrants who plan to stay in the country for a long time, it may be advisable to get to know the place of your choice first during a short trip before arriving directly with all your belongings. If you are short on time or your vacation days for this year are already used up, you can use weekends or bridging days to take a closer look at your potential new place of residence in Spain.

The different regions of Spain

For those who have not yet decided where exactly to live, the choice of regions and places within Spain may seem a bit overwhelming at first. For this reason, I would like to introduce you to the individual regions of Spain in this section and compare them with each other. This way you will get an overview of the different regions and their advantages and disadvantages, cost points, emigration occurrences, and much more. Even if you have already decided on a place in Spain, it can't hurt to think outside the box a bit and get to know the rest of your new home, don't you think?

Andalucía (Andalusia)

Andalusia is one of the most popular regions in Spain for vacationers and emigrants. The region is located in the very south of the Iberian Peninsula and borders the Mediterranean Sea, Gibraltar, the Atlantic Ocean, and the neighboring country Portugal. Andalusia radiates exactly what many imagine when they think of "typical Spanish." Some of the popular dishes in Spain, such as Gazpacho, also come from this region.

Andalusia is known for its strong dialect, which can

sometimes be quite tricky to understand even for Spaniards from other regions. With an unemployment rate of 23.8 % at the end of 2020, Andalusia currently has the highest unemployment rate in mainland Spain. Those who are drawn to Andalusia should also expect high temperatures during the summer months.

Number of expats: high
Cost of living: affordable
Language: Castilian with strong dialect
Average rental price: 9.7 €/m²
Unemployment rate: 19.0 %
Rank of human development in Spain: 14/17
GDP/Capita (EU average=100): 82
Population density (Inhabitants/km²): 92
Capital: Sevilla

Provinces in Andalusia

- Almería
- Cádiz
- Córdoba
- Granada
- Huelva
- Jaén
- Málaga
- Sevilla

Aragón

Aragon is known because of its practical location between the Spanish metropolises of Barcelona and Madrid. Unlike other regions of the country, however, relatively few emigrants live here. The area is particularly known for its Moorish architecture and offers a lot of wonderful nature and hiking opportunities. This is because the Pyrenees already begin in the north of Aragon.

The Aragonese accent is relatively easy to understand and offers only a few deviations from High Spanish, but you will quickly gets used to them. The weather in Aragón differs from the temperatures on the coast. While in some parts, especially in the capital Zaragoza, a strong wind often prevails, Aragón is generally characterized by hot summers and cold winters. Snowfall in winter is also not uncommon here.

Number of expats: low
Cost of living: affordable to medium
Language: Castilian with very slight dialect (Catalan in the border region with Catalonia)
Average rental price: 8.2 €/m²
Unemployment rate: 9.41 %
Rank of human development in Spain: 6/17
GDP/Capita (EU average=100): 112
Population density (Inhabitants/km²): 27
Capital: Zaragoza

Provinces in Aragon

- Huesca
- Teruel
- Zaragoza

Asturias

Asturias is one of the least popular areas of Spain among emigrants. This is despite the fact that it is home to some of the most beautiful beaches in the country. But even tourism is almost mainly limited to local tourists from other parts of Spain.

Asturias has a mild Mediterranean climate, characterized mainly by mild summer temperatures. The area is known for its wonderful pure nature and marvelous landscapes.

Number of expats: very low
Cost of living: affordable
Language: Asturian (Spanish dialect with Galician influences)
Average rental price: 8.0 €/m²
Unemployment rate: 14.39 %
Rank of human development in Spain: 8/17
GDP/Capita (EU average=100): 94
Population density (Inhabitants/km²): 101
Capital: Oviedo

Provinces in Asturias

- Asturias

Islas Baleares (Balearic Islands)

The Balearic Islands are home to some of the most popular islands in the country. Especially the favorite destination of us Germans, the island of Mallorca is in high demand among emigrants.

The islands of Mallorca, Menorca, Cabrera, Ibiza, and Formentera are popular with both Spaniards and foreign tourists. Because gorgeous beaches are waiting here and there is always something going on. Unfortunately, due to their reputations as party islands, Mallorca and Ibiza in particular often have to deal with pollution and over-tourism. However, it does not always have to be loud and crowded. All islands also have a few quiet and secluded places to offer.

Number of expats: very high
Cost of living: costly
Language: Castilian and Catalan
Average rental price: 14.0 €/m²
Unemployment rate: 10.91 %

Rank of human development in Spain: 14/17
GDP/Capita (EU average=100): 115
Population density (Inhabitants/km²): 206
Capital: Palma

Provinces in the Balearic Islands

- Illes Balears

Las Canarias (Canary Islands)

Let's move from the Balearic Islands directly to Spain's next popular island group: The Canary Islands. Although geographically they are actually located at the level of Africa, the Canary Islands politically belong to Spain. Despite that, there are some more differences between the Canary Islands and mainland Spain, not only in terms of taxation.

With their subtropical temperatures and unique nature and beaches on the Atlantic Ocean, the Canary Islands are a popular emigration destination for people from all over the world. Even in winter, temperatures here hardly drop, making the islands a genuine paradise for everyone who doesn't like winter.

Number of expats: very high
Cost of living: costly
Language: Castilian with Canarian dialect
Average rental price: 11.8 €/m²
Unemployment rate: 14.57 %
Rank of human development in Spain: 13/17
GDP/Capita (EU average=100): 95
Population density (Inhabitants/km²): 271
Capital: Las Palmas + Santa Cruz de Tenerife

Provinces in the Canary Islands

- Las Palmas

- Santa Cruz de Tenerife

Cantabria

Cantabria is probably one of the unknown regions of Spain. Located in the north, the region is characterized mainly by beautiful landscapes and mild temperatures. The mild winters and cool summers here are perfect for those not fond of significant temperature fluctuations. In addition to almost endless nature, there are also plenty of ancient caves to discover underground.

Cantabria is located directly on the Cantabrian Sea and offers some fantastic beaches. The accent of the Spanish here is predominantly neutral.

Number of expats: very low
Cost of living: affordable
Language: Castilian
Average rental price: 9.1 €/m²
Unemployment rate: 10.34 %
Rank of human development in Spain: 9/17
GDP/Capita (EU average=100): 104
Population density (Inhabitants/km²): 108
Capital: Santander

Provinces in Cantabria

- Cantabria

Castilla-La Mancha (Castile-La Mancha)

Castile-La Mancha, also known as New Castile, was once an important central place in Spain as part of the historic Castile. Until the 1980s, the capital Madrid was also part of Castile-La Mancha. Covering an area the size of the Czech Republic, this region of Spain has a very low population density (only 4.3 % of Spaniards live here).

Through the story of Don Quixote, Castilla-La

Mancha has become famous all over the world and is still known for its rural landscapes and small villages. Spoken Spanish is considered relatively easy to understand.

Number of expats: low
Cost of living: affordable
Language: Castilian
Average rental price: 6.2 €/m²
Unemployment rate: 14.38 %
Rank of human development in Spain: 16/17
GDP/Capita (EU average=100): 83
Population density (Inhabitants/km²): 25
Capital: Toledo

Provinces in Castile-La Mancha

- Albacete
- Ciudad Real
- Cuenca
- Guadalajara
- Toledo

Castilla y León (Castile and León)

Castile and León also once belonged to Castile and is therefore still often referred to as Old Castile. With its proximity to the capital Madrid, this region is home to some of the most popular day trip destinations in the country. The autonomous region covers an area larger than Portugal, although only 5.7 % of Spain's population lives here.

In general, the area is quiet and full of historic small towns and landmarks. The Spanish spoken in this region is considered the most neutral Spanish in the entire country.

Number of expats: low
Cost of living: affordable
Language: Castilian
Average rental price: 7.2 €/m²
Unemployment rate: 8.83 %
Rank of human development in Spain: 7/17
GDP/Capita (EU average=100): 100
Population density (Inhabitants/km²): 27
Capital: Valladolid

Provinces in Castile and León

- Ávila
- Burgos
- León
- Palencia
- Salamanca
- Segovia
- Soria
- Valladolid
- Zamora

Catalunya – Cataluña (Catalonia)

Catalonia has been in the media repeatedly for years due to its independence protests. Not only the language but also the culture of the Catalans differs in many aspects from the rest of the country.

Catalonia is characterized by its Mediterranean coast, its relatively mild climate, many historic small towns, and modernist architecture. While Spanish is widely spoken, many locals use the second language Catalan. Even in spoken Spanish, there can be frequent mixing of the two official languages.

Number of expats: very high
Cost of living: costly

Language: Castilian and Catalan
Average rental price: 16.0 €/m²
Unemployment rate: 9.91 %
Rank of human development in Spain: 5/17
GDP/Capita (EU average=100): 124
Population density (Inhabitants/km²): 224
Capital: Barcelona

Provinces in Catalonia

- Barcelona
- Tarragona
- Lleida
- Girona

Euskadi – País Vasco (Basque Country)

Just like Catalonia, the Basque Country has its own culture and customs, which may differ from those in the rest of the country. In addition, this region in northern Spain has a second official language, Euskara. The second language is anything but easy to understand - in fact, it is considered one of the most difficult languages in the world to learn.

The Basque Country is considered one of the wealthiest regions in Spain. Euskadi is popular for its beautiful beaches and mild climate, both in winter and summer.

Number of expats: medium
Cost of living: costly
Language: Castilian and Euskara
Average rental price: 12.8 €/m²
Unemployment rate: 8.66 %
Rank of human development in Spain: 2/17
GDP/Capita (EU average=100): 136
Population density (Inhabitants/km²): 296

Capital: Gasteiz/Vitoria

Provinces in the Basque Country

- Araba
- Gipuzkoa
- Bizkaia

Extremadura

This immense region, located on the border with Portugal, is considered one of the poorest in the country. It is also known as one of the regions in Spain with the lowest percentage of immigrants. Extremadura is characterized by small municipalities (57 % of which have fewer than 10,000 inhabitants). This region of Spain has mild, rainy winters and hot, dry summers.

Extremadura is significant in the country for its agriculture because many fruits and vegetables are grown here. Most Extremadura locals speak Spanish with the Extremaduran or Castúo dialect. These are not too different from other southern dialects of Spanish.

Number of expats: very low
Cost of living: very affordable
Language: Castilian with Southern dialect
Average rental price: 5.8 €/m²
Unemployment rate: 17.62 %
Rank of human development in Spain: 17/17
GDP/Capita (EU average=100): 71
Population density (Inhabitants/km²): 26
Capital: Mérida

Provinces in Extremadura

- Badajoz
- Cáceres

Galicia

Galicia is located in the very northwest of the country and has strong ties to Portugal. Its closeness to the neighboring country is especially noticeable in the second official language of the region, as Galician is considered in the middle between Spanish and Portuguese.

Galicia is one of the regions of Spain with excellent access to the sea, as it borders both the Cantabrian Sea and the Atlantic Ocean. Galicia is therefore famous for its beautiful landscapes, cliffs, and rias (estuaries).

Number of expats: low
Cost of living: affordable
Language: Castilian and Galician
Average rental price: 7.8 €/m²
Unemployment Rate: 10.63 %
Rank of human development in Spain: 9/17
GDP/Capita (EU average=100): 88
Population density (Inhabitants/km²): 94
Capital: Santiago de Compostela

Provinces in Galicia

- A Coruña
- Lugo
- Ourense
- Pontevedra

La Rioja

Wine connoisseurs have definitely heard of this Spanish region because La Rioja is one of the finest wine-growing regions in the country. La Rioja is characterized by a mild climate with little rain, just the perfect weather for growing grapes.

Those who move to this region of Spain are probably looking for tranquility, a small town atmosphere, and splendid nature.

Number of expats: low
Cost of living: affordable
Language: Castilian
Average rental price: 7.2 €/m²
Unemployment rate: 8.6 %
Rank of human development in Spain: 4/17
GDP/Capita (EU average=100): 111
Population density (Inhabitants/km²): 62
Capital: Logroño

Provinces in La Rioja

- La Rioja

Madrid

Madrid is not only a city but also the region around the capital of Spain. If you want to live in the center of the country (you can even take that literally in the case of Madrid), Madrid is the right place for you. Madrid is a typical European metropolis, with many events and entertainment options, and an extra dose of Spanish charm. Although Madrid is a modern metropolis, the classical does also play a big part in the city's vibe.

The Spanish spoken in this region is considered the most neutral in the country, along with Castilla y León. Madrid is thus perfect for young people in particular who want to learn Spanish.

Number of expats: very high
Cost of living: costly
Language: Castilian
Average rental price: 15.1 €/m²

Unemployment rate: 11.51 %
Rank of human development in Spain: 1/17
GDP/Capita (EU average=100): 136
Population density (Inhabitants/km²): 755
Capital: Madrid

Provinces in Madrid

- Madrid

Murcia

If you don't like rainy days, Murcia is perfect for you, because with almost 300 days of sunshine a year, this region is considered the driest in all of Europe. Murcia combines a sense of peace and tranquility with some of the country's most beautiful beaches. Winters here are mild, but it can get scorching in summer.

If you don't necessarily want to go to a tourist city like Barcelona or Valencia but still don't want to miss out on sun, beach, and fiesta, Murcia is definitely the place to be. The Spanish spoken here can sometimes feature a strong dialect. Some words used originate from Arabic or Catalan and might be a little challenging to understand for people unfamiliar with the area.

Number of expats: medium
Cost of living: affordable
Language: Castilian with the Murciano dialect
Average rental price: 7.0 €/m²
Unemployment rate: 12.89 %
Rank of human development in Spain: 12/17
GDP/Capita (EU average=100): 89
Population density (Inhabitants/km²): 123
Capital: Murcia

Provinces in Murcia

- Murcia

Navarra (Navarre)

Although this region is relatively small, its landscapes are very different from each other. While the north is part of the Pyrenees, you will find primarily historical sites such as old castles and small villages in the center of Navarre. In the south, on the other hand, you can find beautiful natural landscapes. Just as the landscapes differ, so does the spoken language. Because the closer you get to the border with the Basque Country, the more the Basque language, Euskera, is spoken.

Surprisingly, Navarre is the region in Spain with the lowest unemployment rate at the moment and one of the most prosperous regions in the country.

Number of expats: low - medium
Cost of living: affordable - medium
Language: Castilian and Euskera
Average rental price: 9.3 €/m²
Unemployment rate: 10.09 %
Rank of human development in Spain: 3/17
GDP/Capita (EU average=100): 132
Population density (Inhabitants/km²): 58
Capital: Pamplona

Provinces in Navarre

- Navarra

Comunitat Valenciana (Valencian Community)

Contrary to what many assume, the Valencian Community includes not only the capital Valencia but also two other provinces. The province of Alicante in particular is very popular with emigrants. With its fantastic beaches and mild Mediterranean climate, it particularly attracts retired emigrants to this region. But young people will most certainly not regret moving here.

The second official language in the region is Valencian, mainly used in rural areas and in Valencia itself. However, Spanish is used more and more towards the outer borders (except towards Catalonia).

Number of expats: very high
Cost of living: affordable - medium
Language: Castilian and Catalan (Valencian)
Average rental price: 9.1 €/m²
Unemployment rate: 13.53 %
Rank of human development in Spain: 11/17
GDP/Capita (EU average=100): 96
Population density (Inhabitants/km²): 210
Capital: Valencia

Provinces in the Valencian Community

- Alicante
- Castellón
- Valencia

Ceuta and Melilla

Don't be surprised if you've never heard of these regions of Spain because they are autonomous Spanish exclaves located on the African continent, inside Morocco, to be exact. The autonomous cities are strictly guarded to prevent illegal immigration into the EU.

More than half of the inhabitants in both cities are Muslims. Due to the mixing of cultures and religions and many illegal immigrants, Tarifit is increasingly spoken.

Number of expats: very low (but many illegal immigrants)

Cost of living: affordable

Language: Castilian and Tarifit

Average rental price: 9.3 €/m² in Melilla

Unemployment rate: 30.55 % (Ceuta) & 21.20 % (Melilla)

Rank of human development in Spain: 18 & 19

GDP/Capita (EU average=100): 97 (Ceuta) & 95 (Melilla)

Population density (Inhabitants/km²): 4,127 (Ceuta) & 3,440 (Melilla)

Capital: /

Provinces in Ceuta and Melilla

- Ceuta
- Melilla

The most popular expat destinations in Spain

- Catalonia's Mediterranean Coast
- Valencian Community
- Andalusia
- The Balearic Islands
- Madrid
- The Canary Islands

Regions in Spain at sea

Mediterranean regions in Spain

- Catalonia
- Valencia
- Murcia
- Andalusia

- The Balearic Islands

Regions in the Southern Atlantic

- Andalusia
- Galicia
- The Canary Island

Regions in the Northern Atlantic

- Galicia
- Asturias
- Cantabria
- Basque Country

The coasts of the Spanish Iberian Peninsula

The following regions of Spain have access to at least one coast.

Catalonia's Mediterranean Coast

- Costa Brava
- Costa del Maresme
- Costa del Garraf
- Costa Daurada

Valencia's Mediterranean Coast

- Costa de Azahar
- Costa de Valencia
- Costa Blanca

Murcia' s Mediterranean Coast

- Costa Cálida

Andalusia' s Mediterranean Coast

- Costa de Almería

- Costa Tropical
- Costa del Sol
- Costa Gaditana

Andalusia' s Southern Atlantic Coast

- Costa de la Luz

Galicia' s Northern Atlantic Coast

- Rías Baixas
- Rías Altas

Asturia' s Northern Atlantic Coast

- Costa Verde

Cantabria' s Northern Atlantic Coast

- Costa de Cantabria

Basque Country's Northern Atlantic Coast

- Costa Vasca

Regions in Spain with a second language

In the following, you can see which regions in Spain have a second language besides Castilian Spanish:

- Catalonia
- Balearic Islands
- Valencia
- Basque Country
- The border area of Navarre
- Galicia

The most affordable regions in Spain

The following regions are considered the most

affordable to live in Spain:

- Andalusia
- Asturias
- Cantabria
- Castile-La Mancha
- Castile and León
- Extremadura
- La Rioja
- Murcia
- Ceuta and Melilla

Determine what kind of visa you need for living in Spain

If you don't have an EU passport (which is also the case for UK citizens starting from January 2021), you will most likely need a visa to stay long-term in Spain. There are some exceptions for UK citizens who have lived in Spain pre-Brexit. But in this book, we are assuming you will want to move to Spain now for the first time and have not previously lived there. However, if you do have an EU passport, you don't need a visa to enter and live in Spain. Which means that you can simply skip this step. (Feel free to read the next part anyway to enjoy the fact that you won't have to worry about this.)

If you don't have an EU passport, you might want to check whether there is an option for you to apply for one. If you meet certain criteria, such as being born in an EU member country[16], or having parents or possibly grandparents who emigrated from an EU country to a non-EU country, you might be able to obtain EU citizenship on top of your current citizenship[17]. While the process of proving your right to hold an EU passport might also be connected to some paperwork, it will certainly be worth it. Because moving to Spain without having to worry about work permits and visa renewals can save you quite a bunch of headaches.

However, if you don't have an EU passport and you can't apply for one, you will need to start thinking about your visa at this point. After you have decided what you want to do in Spain and how long you will be staying inside the country, you can already start planning which type of visa you need to apply for to enter and remain in Spain long-term. There are several options to choose from, so it's essential to check in time which visa is suitable for you personally. To help you with that, you can check the flowchart below.

Generally speaking, the main difference between the visas is whether it includes a work permit or not. In the following, I'd like to give you a little overview of the most popular visa options you can apply for. Later in this book, I'll explain where and how to apply for your visa. In any case, you should under no circumstances try to enter Spain on a tourist visa (except if your sole purpose is to visit Spain for a vacation, of course). It's also important to know that remote work while staying in Spain on a tourist visa is not permitted. In general, you can only apply for your initial long-term visa from outside of Spain. So, entering Spain on a tourism visa and trying to apply for a long-term visa from inside the country will most certainly not work. The easiest way will be to apply from a consulate in the country you currently are registered in as a resident.

Depending on your nationality and where you apply for your visa, the processing time might vary. To get an idea, if you apply from the UK as a UK resident, the processing time of your visa will take approximately one to four weeks. You can apply six months before your planned day of entry at the earliest and 20 working days in advance at the latest (however it is recommended you apply earlier). I highly recommend taking a photo or scan and some copies of your passport before the day of your visa application, as your passport will remain in the embassy during the visa processing time. Make sure to check whether you will need an appointment to apply for your visa (most embassies will require you to make an appointment first). If this is the case, make an appointment well in advance to be in good time when applying for your visa. Keep in mind that if you want to move with your family, you will need one appointment for each person.

When handing over the required documents, make sure everything is complete and correctly filled out. While for missing documents, you will most likely be given a certain period of time (up to one month) to complete your documentation or hand in further information; improper or wrongly filled out documents could lead to your visa application being denied. Other reasons for a denial of your visa application could be severe criminal offenses in your criminal record, insufficient private health insurance, an invalid medical health certificate, insufficient financial funds, application for the wrong type of visa, invalid passports, or missing information, among other potential factors. If your visa application gets rejected, you should keep in mind that the embassy will not refund you the processing fee of your visa. That's why it's all the more important to get your documentation right the first time. If your application ends up being rejected, after all, you might still have the option to appeal. This process can lead two ways. You could ask for a "*recurso de reposición*" which is basically asking the embassy to review your application a second time within one month from being rejected. The second option is to ask the superior court of Justice in Madrid (*Tribunal Superior de Justicia de Madrid*) to review your visa application. This process is called "*recurso contensioso administrative.*" You have a timeframe of two months to do so. At that point, you might want to check with a lawyer whether one of these options makes sense for your personal case.

Fig. 1 Spain Long-term Visa Types

Non-Lucrative Visa

A non-lucrative visa is one of the most popular options for foreigners moving to Spain. It's especially popular for retirees moving across the ocean or the channel. Since the non-lucrative visa (*NLV*) doesn't include a working permit, it's arguably the easiest visa to apply for. This visa used to be a popular option for remote workers. However, it turns out that most consulates in the US and UK will now refuse your application if you plan to work remotely. The reason for this is not only the current high unemployment rate in Spain but also the fact that they are currently working on a new type of visa for people working remotely. The new visa is expected to be available for digital nomads and remote workers later this year. Nevertheless, there is not much public information yet about this new visa type. At the end of this visa section, I will tell you a little bit more about it. But let's get back to the NLV for now. As mentioned before, in the post-pandemic world, it's usually pretty challenging to find work in Spain, especially if you are not in the country at the time being. So, the non-lucrative visa can be a good chance to enter Spain and look for a suitable job. Once your visa is up for renewal and you have managed to secure a job offer, you can apply to transition your non-lucrative visa to an employment visa. However, it's crucial that you not start working, whether it's as an employer, freelance, or remote before you have officially received your work permit. Because violating Spanish labor law could have serious consequences, such as a long-term ban on entering the country. Moreover, many countries require you to leave Spain temporarily to pick up your work visa from your country of citizenship.

The Non-Lucrative Visa allows you to stay and reside inside Spain for one year initially. Once the year is up, you can renew the visa for another two years. In total, you can renew the NLV two times. If, after five years, you decide to stay in Spain, you can apply for long-term residency. This long-term residency will be valid for five years and allows you to be treated the same as a Spanish local, such as entitlement to free public healthcare. By moving to Spain, you become a resident of the country, which means that you will have to stay at least 183 days inside the country. As a resident of Spain, you will become liable to pay Spanish income tax which means you will have to pay taxes on your entire world income. It is thus essential to check which taxes you will be required to pay once you live in Spain before moving. Taxes can be pretty complicated, so I highly recommend you talk to a professional before leaving your country. Let me give you an example. Let's say you are a UK citizen who wants to move to Spain long-term. If you sell or bring all your possessions and only live off your savings without receiving any pensions or allowances from your home country (which is quite unrealistic, I know, but please bear with me for the example's sake), you won't be liable to pay taxes in the UK anymore. However, if you are a US citizen doing the same thing, you will still be liable to pay taxes in the US. Many factors can influence your liability of paying taxes in your home country or any other country from which you might receive any form of income. Examples of such factors can be pension payments, real estate you own, remote work, or similar. Furthermore, factors that might influence the amount of taxes you have to pay can be your income, real estate value, your legal status (married, single, etc.), whether you have children, and many more. I hope this clarifies why it's so important to check your personal tax liability before moving abroad as it's impossible to generalize this information.

When applying for your NLV you will have to prove you have sufficient funds in order to keep yourself and your dependents afloat during your stay in the country.

You will need at least € 28,800 in a bank account in your name (+ € 7,200 or more for each dependent joining your visa) or proof of monthly income of at least € 2,400 (+ an additional € 600 per dependent). When renewing your visa, you will have to provide proof of sufficient funds for two years, i.e., double the amount just mentioned, as your visa will be valid for two years. (You might want to keep in mind that the requested amount might be higher at that point in time.) Proof could be a pension plan, a remote work contract, or other types of regular (passive) income streams. In a later part of the book, I will tell you in more detail about the exact requirements and documents you need to apply for the NLV.

Theoretically, you used to be allowed to work remotely for a foreign company. Practically, Spain recently has become much stricter with remote workers. In any case, it's essential to know that if you enter Spain on an NLV, you must not work for a Spanish employer or as a freelancer for a Spanish company. Since you aren't working for a Spanish company or employer, you also won't be entitled to the public health care system of the country. This means that you have to use private medical insurance. You will need to provide proof of your insurance when applying for your visa. This means it's vital to find suitable medical insurance for yourself and your dependents well in advance.

Ok, that was a lot of information to take in. So, let's recap the whole thing. The following key data apply to the Non-Lucrative Visa:

- You can reside inside the country for one year – afterward, you can renew your visa two times for two years each (after that, you can apply for long-term residency)
- You must stay inside the country for at least 183

days per year
- You are not allowed to work in Spain (i.e., for a Spanish company or a Spanish employer)
- You are not allowed to start your own company, branch, or work as a freelancer within Spain
- You won't be able to access the Spanish public healthcare system – which means you will need to get private health insurance
- You will be liable for Spanish income tax
- You can include dependents on your visa, such as your spouse, your children, or parents in need of care

Residence Visa for Employees

As we have already discussed in this book, finding work in Spain as a non-European foreigner is not particularly a walk in the park. But if you do manage to find a job in Spain, you have the option to apply for a work permit visa. This type of visa allows you to work inside the country as an employee for a local business (*"por cuenta ajena"*) and get access to the Spanish healthcare system. However, this process is easier said than done as the employment visa comes with its difficulties. In other words, it can be a long, nerve-racking process to get everything figured out. Due to the high unemployment rate in Spain, local employers are only allowed to employ either highly qualified workers from outside of the EU or fill job positions from the list of occupations of difficult coverage[18]. This list is updated quarterly by the Ministry of Public Employment and includes job positions difficult to fill with local workers. In short, you can apply for a work visa if you either have a specific job title of higher education or your future employer has previously unsuccessfully tried to fill the job position with a local or EU citizen. Unfortunately, the employment type of visa comes with a lot of paperwork for you and your future employer. Besides proving that they couldn't fill the position with a local worker, your employer will also have to prove possession of sufficient funds needed for the project you will be employed for. Because it would be quite nice if they were able to pay you for your work, right? Besides that, the employer has to be enrolled in the Social Security system for you to get access to it once you start working. If all these boxes are checked, your future employer first needs to request an official entry allowance for you before you can start your visa process. This entry permission is needed when you apply for your work visa. Only once they have obtained your entry permission can you begin the visa application process. As you see, the whole process is not quite a piece of cake and can take up to eight months. With all this draining paperwork, you will certainly need a lot of patience to get through it. Once you arrive in Spain and begin your work, you will be able to access the country's public healthcare system. As a Spanish resident, you will now be liable to pay income tax. Before leaving, make sure to check whether and what types of taxes must still be paid in your home country when living abroad. Another critical point to keep in mind is when entering Spain on a visa for employees, you are not permitted to work as a freelancer or start your own company. In any case, if you are only going to work for a short-term or temporary job, you might want to look into the work visa for seasonal work instead.

In summary, the following key data apply to the Residence Visa for Employees[19]:

- You can reside inside the country and work as an employee for a local employer
- Your employer must prove that you are either a

highly qualified professional or they have previously unsuccessfully tried to fill the job positions with an EU-member
- Your employer must be enrolled in the Spanish Social Security system and have sufficient economic means for the project you are being employed for
- You must have sufficient professional qualifications for the job you are being employed for
- Before applying for an employment visa, your (future) employer must have requested and obtained official authorization for you to reside and work in Spain
- The payment of your job must meet certain criteria and be above a minimal salary[20]
- You are not allowed to start your own company, branch, or work as a freelancer
- You will be liable for Spanish income tax
- Your dependents can file a separate application for the Residence Visa (non-lucrative)

Residence Self-Employment Visa

If your desired job is not part of the list of occupations of difficult coverage, why not create your own job? Well, to be honest, it's not going to be that easy, but if you have a promising business plan and the necessary funds for turning it into reality, it's totally doable. Nevertheless, unlike the visa option for employees, you won't be able to rely on your employer to request the obligatory paperwork for you. So, you have to make sure to come prepared. Once your visa has been approved, you can reside and work in Spain ("*por cuenta propia*") on a freelance basis. However, like any other visa, this one comes with its own conditions, and to be completely honest with you, it's not that easy. For one, you must be at least 18 years of age to work as a freelancer in Spain.

The crucial element is your business plan. So your business approach should already be well established at the time of your application. The more details you can provide and the better and more secure your business idea, the higher your chances of being approved. A big, big plus point is if your business will create new job opportunities for locals on-site. Are you planning to hire someone or create any type of job for locals? Make sure to mention that in your business plan. You can add any kinds of important documents such as building leases, rental contracts, or similar. Besides a great idea and a well-elaborated plan, you will also need to provide proof of sufficient funds for your business and cover your own living cost in the country. To cover your overall expenses, you will need to demonstrate a bank balance of at least € 28,800 in it or proof of monthly income of at least € 2,400. Besides that, you will have to provide evidence that you can afford to implement your business plan on-site. The required amount of money will depend on the nature of your business. Such evidence can be your own private savings, income streams, or other types of funding like loans or third-party investments. Besides money, another fundamental factor is your personal preparation and education. Because not only do you have to provide a great business plan but also prove that you are qualified to actually put your plan into action and conduct your business. Such qualifications can be business degrees, training, or further education you have received. If all this goes well and your application is approved, you will be allowed to enter Spain and start your business. However, once you arrive in the country, you will need to register your business correctly on-site. Under the section *How to register as an autónomo*, I will tell you how. After entering Spain, you will become liable for Spanish income tax. If you provide any type of service or sell products to your clients, you will also have to pay Spanish valued tax

(*IVA*). I recommend you use the services of a tax attorney or professional company to get help with your taxes until you get the hang of it. These services are usually quite affordable in Spain and start at € 10 a month.

Ok, so let's summarize all this info. The following key data apply to the Residence Visa for Self-Employment[21]:

- You can reside inside the country and work as a freelancer or start your own business
- Must be 18 years old or older
- You will have to provide a business plan such as proof of sufficient funds for your project
- You must have sufficient professional qualifications for the project you are planning to pursue
- You will be liable for Spanish income tax
- After entering Spain, you will need to register yourself and your business with the local authorities (I'll explain how later in this book)
- Your dependents can fill a separate application for the Residence Visa (non-lucrative)

Student Visa

As you might be able to guess from its name, this visa is meant for students who want to study in Spain. You can apply for a student visa if you are either accepted to study full-time at an official University in Spain, school, or an officially recognized (by Cervantes Institute) Spanish language school or a language school teaching another of the official languages in Spain such as Catalan or Galician.

The following key data apply to the Student Visa[22]:

- You must be accepted for full-time study at one of

the official Universities or schools in Spain

- Or you must be accepted at one of the official language schools in Spain
- Or have any corresponding documents that prove your involvement in an unpaid internship, student exchange, or voluntary work
- You can reside in Spain during the period of your studies
- You are not allowed to work in Spain
- You must have and prove sufficient funds for financing your stay in the country (the required amount differs between consulates of different countries)

Golden Visa

Your piggy bank is filled to the brim, and you have no idea what to invest in? Great! Then this visa seems to be the perfect fit for you. Also known as an investment visa, the golden visa option is meant for people planning to invest in Spanish companies, funds, or real estate. In any case, to obtain this visa, the investment can not be too small – you have to:

- Buy real estate worth € 500,000 or more
- Or possess 1 million € worth of shares of a Spanish company
- Or 2 million € value of Spanish public debt securities
- Or 1 million € in Spanish investment funds

Family Member of an EU-Citizen Visa

The name of this visa says it all. If you want to apply for this type of visa, you must be related to an EU-citizen or have an EU member in your family. By family, we are not only talking about your literal family but also your family-in-law who is usually your spouse. That means that you can apply for this kind of visa if you are married or in a long-term relationship with an EU member. If you are not legally married, make sure to go through the "*pareja de hecho*" process first, in which you register your relationship with the Spanish civil registry office. You can find a guide to this process in the links in the end of the book[23]. If your partner is a citizen of another EU-state, you will need to register your relationship in his or her state. In short, the following people can make use of the Family Member of an EU-citizen visa[24]:

- The spouse of an EU member
- Your or your spouse's children until the age of 21 if one of you is an EU member
- Your or your spouse's parents who are in your or your spouse's care if one of you is an EU member

Family Reunification Visa

You or your spouse have already legally lived in Spain for more than a year, and now you would like to live there together? Then this visa might be the right fit for you. Under the family regrouping visa, you will be able to bring your close family, i.e., your spouse, children, or spouse's children, and possibly parents or parents-in-law in need of care, with you to Spain. However, to do so, one of you must have legally resided in the country for at least one year and have previously renewed your initial residence visa. The following members of your family can apply for the family reunification visa if the previously discussed conditions are met and you have previously lived in Spain for at least one year[25]:

- Your spouse or registered partner

- Your or your spouse's children until 18 years of age (there might be an exception made until the age of 21 if you can prove the child depends on you financially)
- Your or your spouse's children over the age of 18 with disabilities
- Your parents or your parents-in-law over the age of 65 (there might be an exception made for younger parents if you can prove their need for care)

EU Blue Card

If you are a highly qualified worker and want to work in Spain or other EU member countries, you also have the option to apply for the EU Blue card. In general, the EU Blue card can be seen as the EU version of the US Green Card. Once you meet all the criteria regarding the EU Blue card, you can apply for it, travel freely within the EU, and even bring your close family with you. Each of the EU members (exceptions are Ireland and Denmark) have different conditions regarding this visa, such as minimum threshold salary and residency time issued with this visa. While the following key data only represents the EU Blue card issued in Spain, you can check the conditions for other EU members in 2022 in our further links below[26]. Your (future) employer can help you apply for this visa. The idea is to stay at least 18 months in the job you initially applied for. After that, you are free to change to another high-quality position within the EU. But don't forget that if you want to work in another country while being an EU Blue cardholder, you will need to meet the minimum threshold salary of the country you are planning to move to. A significant advantage of this visa compared to the regular working visa for Spain is that you can apply for long-term residency after five years even if you have changed the country you live in during these five years (as long as that country is an EU member, of course). In any case, the following key points should be met if you want to apply for the EU Blue card for working and residing in Spain[27]:

- You have a high-quality job contract or binding job offer for at least one year
- You will earn at least € 33,908 per year with this job
- You hold the required job title in order to carry out this job (for regulated professions)
- For a non-regulated job, you must have higher professional qualifications, e.g., a university title
- Spain and a few other EU members also allow five years of professional high-level work experience to be counted as higher professional qualifications[28]
- The Spanish EU Blue card is valid for one year (Card Fee: € 418; Each renewal: € 112)
- If you lose your job, you are given a period of three months to find a new job before your Blue card is withdrawn

Digital Nomad Visa

2023 comes with a lot of changes in the Spanish bureaucratic system. One of those is the long-awaited Digital Nomad visa. Its appearance has been postponed several times throughout the last year, but since the end of December 2022, it's now finally available. This new visa is not only for digital nomads in the literal sense but also for remote workers wanting to start a long-term life in Spain. Even the application process has been adapted to the needs of digital nomads, as you can apply directly from within the country while staying on a tourist visa. By doing so, you can receive a 3-year residence permit which can later be renewed for two additional years.

After five years, you can apply for permanent residency. If you apply from your local embassy outside of Spain, you will receive a one-year residency permit. However, once you arrive, it can also be transferred to a 3-year permit. Another benefit of this visa is its fast issuing time. While other visa types might need several months to be approved, the digital nomad visa is designed to be approved within 20 working days. Don't worry if you don't hear back from them once the 20 days have passed because, in this case, silence means your visa application has been approved. The residency permits issued on this visa can later be used for applying for permanent residency (after five years) or citizenship (after ten years). If you travel with your family, you can also include them in your visa application, so that they can receive a residency permit as well. Once you have your permit, you are free to travel within the EU.

Nevertheless, like any visa, also this one comes with its limits. While the digital nomad visa allows you to work for foreign companies and clients, it's crucial to know that your income base from inside the country cannot exceed 20 % of your total income. This means that you could theoretically work for Spanish companies or with Spanish clients as long as at least 80 % of your income is generated outside of the country. If you stay in the country for more than 183 days a year, you automatically become a Spanish tax resident. But since the visa has been created to attract foreign entrepreneurs to Spain, it comes with serval tax incentives. Basically, the tax model that will apply to you is an optimized version of the so-called Beckham law, which we will discuss in a couple of minutes. Let me sum it up for you - if you have not lived or visited Spain in the past five years, you have the option to pay a flat tax rate of only 24 % of your income. Depending on the income you generate, the general progressive tax rate used in Spain could reach as much as 48 %. So this visa's tax incentive could possibly be a big money saver for you. This law includes income of up to € 600,000. But hold on, that's not all. Staying on this visa will also free you from the need to pay wealth taxes in Spain or fill out the modelo 720 for asset declarations abroad.

If you want to take advantage of these tax benefits, it's crucial that you apply to be considered a non-resident for tax purposes within the first six months after receiving your visa. If you are unsure whether it's best to apply for this, consult a gestor or tax advisor. They can also help you with the application process.

Ok, that has been a lot of information, so let's resume the key features of this visa[29]:

- You can reside inside the country, work as a freelancer for foreign clients, or work remotely for a foreign company.
- The company you work for or have relations with must be located outside Spain.
- Your income generated from Spanish clients or companies cannot be more than 20 %.
- You must prove that you have worked with your company or clients for at least three months prior to your visa application.
- The company you work for must have existed at least one year before your application.
- Your contract must state that you are allowed to work remotely from abroad.
- You will be liable for Spanish income tax.
- You must submit a clean criminal record certificate (for at least five years).
- You must hire private health insurance with full coverage in the country.
- You must prove sufficient financial means for yourself and each dependent, which means 200 % of the local minimum wage (€ 25,000) and 75 % for

each dependent (€ 9,441).
- You must correctly fill out the application form[30].
- You must pay the corresponding visa fee.

More visa options

If your plan for living in Spain doesn't fit any of the visas mentioned above, don't worry. There are a couple more visa options that might suit you better. You can check the different options with the Spanish Ministry of Foreign Affairs or your local consulate[31].

The insurance issue

When moving to Spain, be sure to clarify how you want to be insured during your time in the country. Make sure you are not without insurance at any time. Health insurance in particular is indispensable.

After you have decided how long you want to stay in Spain, the question of insurance is usually easy to solve. The most essential thing when looking for suitable health insurance is to check with your embassy or consulate. This is because some visa options have certain requirements on which type of insurance you need. If you're going to spend only a few months or up to a year in the country, international insurance can be worthwhile. However, this type of insurance is usually not accepted by authorities issuing your visa.

To be on the safe side, and especially if you plan to stay in the country for a more extended period, you should definitely take out Spanish insurance. If you work in Spain as an employee, the health insurance (in this case *Seguridad Social*) is free of charge for you. Your children can also be insured through you up to the age of 26.

The health care system in Spain works differently than in the US and the UK. For example, private health insurance is necessary if you want to have access to private medical practices. However, these are usually much more affordable than what we are used to from our home countries. You will learn more about this topic in a later part of the book.

Pension entitlements abroad

If you plan to stay in Spain for an extended period of time, or if you plan to leave for Spain as a retiree, it is crucial to find out about your pension rights abroad before you go.

Even though you may be young now and see your pension in the distant future, it is still essential to know whether and to what extent you are entitled to your paid-in pension contributions when you live abroad. However, as a rule, there are usually no problems in claiming the pension payments from your home country while living in Spain. You should definitely contact your pension provider before leaving to get detailed information about your pension entitlement.

In general, pension contributions paid from other countries must be taxed in Spain if you are registered as a resident in the country, which is the case after more than 183 days of residence. Whether the pension must also be taxed in your home country is determined by different factors, such as your current residency situation. In Spain, however, foreign pension payments are taxed at the national income tax rate (IRPF). It is essential that you seek advice from a specialist on this matter before leaving for Spain. More information on tax agreements between the USA and Spain can be found in the links below[32] as well as for the UK[33].

Suppose you reach the age of at least 65[*2] and have paid into the Spanish social security system for at least

---

[2] In Spain, the retirement age is being raised to 67 in stages.

15 years (at least two of them immediately before retirement). In this case, you are entitled to receive a regular Spanish old-age pension (*jubilación ordinaria*). The amount of pension paid depends on your previous income ("*the calculation base*") and the number of years paid in. Starting with 15 years of contributions, you will receive 50 % of the calculation base. From there, the percentage increases per year paid in until it reaches 100 % at 35 years and six months paid in. Other options for the Spanish pension are the Flexible Pension (*Jubilación flexible*) or Partial Pension (*Jubilación parcial*). Detailed information and an application for these options can be made through Social Security (*Seguridad Social*).[34]

Language skills

On emigration forums and groups, this question comes up all the time: "*Do I really need to learn Spanish if I live in Spain?*" Before I answer this question, I would first like to ask you a few short counter questions:

- Do you want to spend your entire time in Spain not being able to communicate?
- Do you want to make acquaintances with locals and really get to know the culture and traditions of the country?
- Do you want to integrate?
- Do you want to always have to rely on someone who happens to speak English in case of an emergency?
- Do you want to be able to ask where the milk is at the supermarket?
- Do you want to be able to ask for help in an emergency?
- Would you like to always have to rely on a translator for bureaucratic matters?
- Do you want to be able to understand all the terms

and conditions when signing contracts?

Perhaps after reading these questions, it is already clear to you what I am getting at. Now to the question: If you emigrate to tourist areas, like my hometown Barcelona or Majorca, you can usually get by without Spanish. You can also find a job without knowing Spanish and work with other emigrants there. It is possible to build an international circle of friends without speaking a word of Spanish. But do you really want to do that?

Isn't the whole point of moving abroad to integrate into the new country, adopt new customs and fully engage with life in Spain? The level of English in Spain is very low, at least outside of tourist areas. If you don't want to go beyond that, you can get by without knowing Spanish. But if you plan to dive deeper into the Spanish way of life, you simply must be able to understand it.

Without Spanish, you will probably only be a guest in the country even after years. But if you make an effort to learn at least the basic vocabulary of the Spanish language, you will connect much faster and get to know real Spanish life.

Castilian

If you have studied Spanish in Latin America, you will quickly notice that the Spanish spoken in Spain (Castilian) is different from the Spanish spoken there.

You can think of these differences as a (strong) dialect, much like the difference between Oxford English and the English spoken in the US. Especially when it comes to food, polite phrases, and speed of speech, spoken Spanish differs in various countries. However, as with any dialect, it will certainly only take you a short time to get used to new words and different pronunciation.

Four striking differences between Castilian and Latin American Spanish

Usted: While Latin Americans usually address each other as *usted* or *vos* ("you"), in Spain people usually address each other in a less formal way using *tú*.

Hostia Tio and Vale: In South America there is a not entirely serious rule of thumb according to which you can always recognize Spaniards by their frequent use of the expressions "*Hostia, Tio*" (means something like "wow, man") and *vale* ("ok").

Z: While the Spanish pronounce the Z like an English *th*, in Latin America it is pronounced like a sharp s.

Coger: While in Spain, we translate the verb *coger* as "to take" (e.g., *to take the bus*), in South America, it can mean something like "*to have sex*," and therefore tends to cause some confusion.

Other languages in the country

Although *Castellano* (Castilian) has been established as the official language in the country, some autonomous regions of Spain each have another recognized official language on top of this. In total, there are three or four other languages officially spoken and taught in parts of the country: Catalan, Basque, Galician (and Valencian).

Although many residents of Spain have a second or another native language, the percentage of Spaniards who do not speak Spanish is thus very small. During the

Spanish Franco dictatorship (1936 - 1975), it was even forbidden by law in the country to use other languages except for Castilian. As a result, today many Spaniards in the older generation understand the second official language of their region but cannot use it in writing.

Catalan

Catalan is the language officially recognized as the second official language alongside Castilian in the autonomous region of Catalonia. However, a dialect of Catalan is also spoken in the Balearic Islands. The differences between Catalan in Catalonia and Catalan in the Balearic Islands can be considered similar to the differences between the various dialects in English. The dialects also differ on the individual islands and are known as Mallorcan, Menorcan, and Ibizan. But also, spoken Catalan differs between the regions on the mainland. In general, the biggest difference between the various dialects is the pronunciation of unstressed vowels. Following this rule, Catalan is even further divided into Eastern Catalan and Western Catalan. Outside of Spain, Catalan is also spoken in Andorra, part of the Pyrenees region of France, and by some inhabitants of the town of Alghero in Sardinia - a true world language.

Some Spaniards like to refer to Catalan as the "*Polish of Spain*" since the pronunciation and grammatical rules of the language may well sound like an Eastern European language to non-Catalans. In general, Catalan resembles Spanish but is spoken in a much more nasal manner and has strong influences from French. If we now add a few slightly confusing grammar rules and funny accents, we will reach the Catalan language.

Valencian

Valencian is the second official language in the autonomous region of Valencia. Although Valencian is considered the region's official language, many linguists and people internationally consider it a dialect or variety of Catalan rather than a language in its own right. Since Valencians, like Catalans, often have a great deal of national pride, you may not want to broach the subject of whether Valencian is a language or not over lunch with a Valencian.

Galician

The Galician language (Gallego) is considered the second official language in the autonomous region of Galicia. It is also used in some neighboring localities such as Asturias, León, and Zamora. While Catalan has French influences, Galician is strongly related to Portuguese. The language is therefore even considered by some to be in between Spanish and Portuguese.

While Catalan and Basque are understood by only about 60 % of the population in their respective regions due to immigration, the number of Galician speakers in Galicia is much higher (close to 90 %).

In general, the language is further divided into three different dialect groups: Eastern Galician, Central Galician, and Western Galician.

Basque

Basque (Euskara) is another of the three or four minority languages in Spain. It is used in the Basque Country and parts of Navarre. Outside Spain, the Basque language is also used in the French border region of Biscay. While Catalan and Galician have Romance roots like Spanish, Basque has nothing in common with Spanish. But not only does Basque have no relationship with Spanish, it also has no relationship with any other

European language. The Basque language is thus currently the only language in Europe not related to any other. Although there are various hypotheses about its origin and relationship, the language's ancestry has not yet been clearly established. Basque is also further subdivided into about 25 dialects, depending on the region, although the various dialects usually differ only slightly from each other.

However, anyone who decides to learn the Basque language should know beforehand that it is considered one of the most difficult languages to learn in the world. This is not only because no genetic connections can be made to other languages but also because of the complicated grammatical endings of the language. But precisely because the language is so unique, it is all the more important to preserve it and pass it on. So, if you have chosen this region of Spain as your new home and have learned the basics of the language, feel free to send me an email so that I can refund the price of this book as a token of my respect.

Organize the transport of your furniture

Unless you're moving out of your already furnished student apartment, you'll certainly have some furniture and items you'd like to take with you or get rid of.

First of all, you should declutter a bit and find out what is worth taking with you and what would be better leaving at home. If you are only emigrating for a certain period of time, you also have the option of storing your belongings somewhere in the meantime until you return home. If you cannot keep your belongings with friends or relatives, renting a garage or storage room may be worthwhile.

However, if you want to live in Spain for a more extended period of time, you basically have two options:

- o Selling or giving away your furniture
- o   Hiring a shipping company to transport your furniture to Spain

Of course, you can also make the whole thing depend on the price. Maybe it is cheaper to buy an already furnished apartment in Spain? So compare different companies and think carefully about which option you want to choose.

Accommodation issues

Another critical point you should think about before emigrating is the question of where you will live. Do you want to live in a rented apartment, move into a shared apartment, or maybe even buy a property? Depending on the location and your options, there are different ways to find a suitable place to live.

In big cities, such as Barcelona and Madrid, it is a good idea to book a hotel or Airbnb room for the first few days and look for a suitable apartment on-site, as apartments and rooms are usually allocated within a few days. It can therefore be challenging to find an apartment in advance.

If you want to buy a property in the country, you must first apply for a Spanish identity number, known as NIE. This is a Spanish tax number required for some processes in the country. You can apply for the NIE before arriving in the country through the Spanish consulate or after arriving in the country. But don't worry, in a later chapter, you will learn more about the NIE.

But it's not only in Spain where you should take care of a rental contract, because you should also terminate your rental contract in your home country to get out of your contract on time. To play it safe, find out about the notice period specified in your lease a few months in advance. Nothing is more annoying than having to pay rent for two places at once later.

Terminate contracts

In addition to your rental contract, you probably have a few other contracts that you will no longer need after moving to another country. Such contracts can be club or gym fees, electricity, water, internet, magazine or newspaper subscriptions, mobile and telephone contracts, and insurance.

You should therefore look through all your contracts in good time and note the notice periods. This is the only way to cancel your contracts early and on time. If you're not sure whether you are aware of all your different contracts, just check your account history to see which companies regularly debit your premiums.

Extra tip: If you end up overlooking a contract and therefore did not cancel it in time, you can enclose a copy of your deregistration certificate from your home country with your notice of cancellation. Some providers are accommodating and will waive further payments. However, it would be best if you did not rely on this just in case because, well, you know, companies often care more about the money than making their (future) ex-customers happy.

Check documents for completeness

If you want to move abroad, you will of course need valid documents. These can be identity papers, such as an identity card or passport, contracts, birth certificate, marriage certificate, employment certificates or proof of education and training, vaccination certificates, or similar. Different documents are necessary depending on how (long) you want to live in Spain.

You should therefore check your documents for completeness and, if necessary, have them translated into Spanish.

In addition, you should not only concern yourself with the documents you need to obtain in your country. Because it can also be practical to apply for a Spanish identity number, the NIE, before you arrive in Spain and find out about the process of applying for other essential documents locally. But don't worry, this book is designed to prepare you perfectly for the upcoming battle with the Spanish red tape.

Career matters

Of course, you should also consider what exactly you want to do with your life once you have arrived in Spain. In the simplest case, you will have moved to Spain as a pensioner or student. However, if you are part of the working population, you have several options:

- Self-employment (Autónomo)
- Being employed by a Spanish company
- In the employment of an international company
- Start your own business

Good preparation is the key if you want to start working immediately after arriving in Spain. You will also need to have all your documentation ready once you apply for your visa. It's important to know that you will need to apply for a work visa if you want to do any type of work while you are in Spain, be it working as an employer, remote, or self-employed. Furthermore, self-employed work in Spain must be registered a maximum of 30 days after beginning the activities. In addition, you must pay fees for self-employment in Spain from the first month. The amount of the fees differs by various factors, such as your gender and age. An NIE is required to register your activities. You can find more detailed information about the NIE and registering self-employed activities in Spain later in this book.

In big cities like Barcelona in particular, English-speaking employees are always wanted for sales and customer service for various companies. While these jobs are easy to get compared to many other types of work, they usually offer little opportunity for your personal development and unfortunately more often than not also pay poorly. However, such jobs can be a valuable way to get a foothold in Spain, get a work visa, and earn some initial money while looking for a more suitable job. This way, you don't spend all your savings right away and can instead keep them on hand as collateral.

Suppose you plan to continue working in your profession in Spain. In this case, it is crucial to find out whether your professional training is recognized in Spain or whether further steps are necessary before you are allowed to start working. In any case, you should have certificates of education and training translated into Spanish by a certified translator.

Recognition of degrees and professional training

Anyone who has already completed a course of study, training, further education, or has several years of work experience before moving to Spain and would like to continue practicing their learned profession in Spain should definitely find out whether their professional training will be recognized in their new home country.

Especially for medical professionals, architects, lawyers, and similar professions, recognition of the professional education (*Homologación*) is required to be allowed to work in Spain. If you are not sure whether your profession is one of these jobs, you can check with the National Assistance Centre for the Recognition of Professional Qualifications by sending an email to *asistencia.directiva@universidades.gov.es*[35]. To have your professional education recognized, you need the *Solicitud de equivalencia de título extranjero de educación superior*[36]. This document must be submitted to the authorities together with your title and its certified translation. If you want to have your title recognized before arriving in Spain, the nearest Spanish consulate or embassy is the right place to go. If you have already arrived in Spain, your home country's nearest consulate or embassy is responsible for you.

Depending on the title, different fees are due. The recognition of a university title[37], for example, currently costs € 166.50. Please note that the price is based on the number of titles to be recognized and not on the number of applications. The fee can be paid either by bank transfer or by using the document Tasa 107 (Modelo 790)[38]. You can, of course, also have non-university professional titles recognized.[39]

Check your taxes

Taxes can be quite a complicated topic as it doesn't only involve your home country's tax laws but also the tax regulations in Spain. You can never get too much information about taxes when moving abroad. So, make sure to start early on. If you don't speak Spanish yet – and I mean speaking well enough actually to understand public information on taxes – I highly recommend you schedule a meeting with a tax consultant or a person familiar with the topic. So many things can influence where and how many taxes have to be paid that it would be impossible for me to give you more than just some general info at this point. Things that can influence your taxes could be your assets, income, legal status, children, where you live, where you are from, and many more factors. Most of the long-term visas for Spain require you to become a tax resident in the country. This means that you will have to pay taxes on your world income. If your country has a tax treaty with Spain[40] (like the US and the UK), you usually don't have to worry about paying double taxes. Depending on the type of income you receive and the type of work you do, you will have to submit your tax return quarterly or annually. There are many (English-speaking) tax consultants and what are called gestorías throughout the country and online that can help you with it. In my experience, the process is fairly easy.

One thing very important to know for US citizens is that no matter what kind of assets you have in the US and how long you have lived abroad, once you have a US passport or green card, you will always be considered a US tax resident. This means that you will always have to file taxes in the US even if you move abroad and become a tax resident of Spain.

The Spanish income tax

The most important tax you will have to know about when moving to Spain is the Spanish income tax (*IRPF*). The IRPF tax rate is calculated according to the amount of your world income and currently ranges from 19 % to 47 %. Determining the percentage you will have to pay happens in steps, e.g., if you earn between € 12,450 and € 20,199 annually as an employee, you will have to pay 24 %, while if you make between € 20,200 and € 35,199, you will have to pay 30 %. You can find the current IRPF tax rates for 2022/2023 in the links below[41]. However, since so many factors influence the amount of taxes, tax-free allowances, and deductibles, it doesn't make sense to get much deeper into it at this point. I recommend you talk to a tax consultant when submitting your tax return (for the first time).

Modelo 720

One thing to be aware of is the Modelo 720[42]. In this informative tax declaration, you need to file all the assets you own abroad with a value or generated income higher than € 50,000. Such assets could be real estate, shares, foreign bank accounts, properties, or other types of financial products. The Modelo 720 is not meant for paying taxes but is solely meant for informational purposes. However, this doesn't necessarily mean that you won't have to pay taxes on those assets later on.

This tax declaration has to be handed in every year between 01st January and the 31st March. Failure to do so or not declaring assets can be punished with fees starting from € 10,000 (€ 5,000 for each missing asset). If you use the services of a tax consultant to declare Modelo 720, it might be recommendable to use the same professional when submitting your general tax return as both declarations should align.

Spanish non-resident tax

If you are not considered a resident in Spain but still own assets in the country, you are liable for Spanish non-resident taxes. So, if you use a newly acquired property as a vacation home but officially still live somewhere else and are liable for paying taxes there, you should be aware that despite everything, taxes will be due in Spain. However, due to the double tax treaty between the UK and Spain, no further income taxes will probably be expected in the UK for UK residents if you do not rent out your Spanish property. Make sure to check with an independent tax advisor about your tax situation and where and how your taxes will be charged to you personally. There is also a double tax treaty between the USA and Spain in place. Since US citizens are always obligated to pay taxes in the US, even if they live abroad, it is highly advisable to check with an expert about how to file your taxes in the US as well as in Spain[43].

As a non-resident property or general asset owner, you are obliged to pay the annual non-resident tax Modelo 210 (*Impuesto sobre la Renta de no Residentes*). You can either fill out and submit the Modelo 210 document yourself (you can find the document in the links below[44]) or get help from an (Englishspeaking) tax advisor or a specialized company. The tax rate is currently 19 % for EU citizens and 24 % for non-EU citizens but fluctuates periodically. The taxes are due in the respective following year until 31/12. So, if you buy a property this year, 2023, the tax declaration must be made by 31.12.2024. It is best to find out in good time when the last working day before 31.12 is so as not to exceed the deadline.

Wealth taxes

Another thing you should be aware exists in Spain is wealth taxes (*Impuesto de Patrimonio*). It's definitely important to know that this tax will affect both residents and non-residents, i.e., people gaining assets in Spain. For residents, the wealth tax will be charged for the net amount of their world assets, including income streams and possession from outside the country. However, some exceptions won't be included in the Spanish wealth tax, such as pension rights or shareholdings in family companies. It's crucial to know that this tax will be charged on top of your general income taxes. However, if you don't have assets higher than € 700,000, you won't need to pay this tax. Additionally, if you are a resident of Spain, you also receive a € 300,000 tax-free allowance on your own property. The amount of taxes you will be charged depends on the number of your assets and the region you live in. It generally ranges between 0.2 and 3.5 %.

Beckham Law

If, by hearing the name of this Spanish tax law, the first thing you think of is the soccer player David Beckham, you are exactly right. As one of the first people to take advantage of this Spanish tax-saving method, the law has been named after him. The Beckham Law has been in place for almost twenty years now and has been issued to attract (wealthy) expats to Spain. If you apply to be taxed after this law, you can live in Spain and still be taxed as a non-resident. For you, this basically means that instead of paying, let's say, 30 % on the € 34,000 you earn from within the country, you will only be charged 24 %. So, if the Beckham Law is applied to you, you only pay a flat rate of 24 % on your Spanish income during your first six years living in Spain instead of paying 19 to 47 % on your world income. However, while it sounds great at first, not having to pay taxes for your world income in Spain does not mean you won't have to pay taxes in the country where this income is created. But if you do move to Spain on an averagely high-paid job contract, you might want to look into this law as it can save you a lot of taxes. However, you must apply within six months of signing in with Social Security in order to benefit from it. You can do so by filling out the Modelo 149[45]. You can apply to be taxed under the Beckham law if you

- Have a binding job offer in Spain with a Spanish company
- Moved to Spain within the last six months
- Have not been resident in Spain within the last ten years
- Don't gain more than 15 % of your income from abroad

This, in return, means that freelancers and entity directors cannot apply to be taxed under this law. But if you meet the criteria, this law could be very beneficial in helping you save taxes during your first few years in the country. However, this law also comes with its downsides. Since you will be taxed as a non-resident, you won't be able to make use of double taxation agreements between Spain and the countries in which you generate income. Moreover, you will still be taxed for Spanish properties and capital gains in Spain. Furthermore, this law only applies to revenue of up to € 600,000.

Moving to Spain with kids

If you are not moving abroad alone, but together with your children, there are even more issues you need to consider. Because the little ones are not always as convinced about the move as the adults. It may well be understandable that it is not easy to leave your familiar surroundings and get used to a new place, culture, and language. Talking to expat parents, I learned that most children needed about four months to get used to the new language, slowly follow lessons at school, and make new friends.

Science agrees with these numbers. According to statistics, it takes about six months to a year and a half for children to understand or even become fluent in the new language. The exact time depends on each individual child and to what extent they interact with the new language. Depending on your child's personality, extracurricular activities with local children can also be a great way to become familiar with the new language. Irene, an immigrant who had moved from German-speaking Switzerland to Spain at the age of ten with her three siblings and her parents, told me how comfortable she and her siblings had felt after moving to Spain. She explained that the locals received them with open arms and welcomed them into their midst. Further, she revealed that the younger siblings had far fewer problems with the language than the older ones. However, this is not necessarily because young children can learn language faster, but rather because children are less afraid of making mistakes in pronunciation and thus automatically practice much more. Older children, much like us adults, are often shy of the new language because they want to avoid embarrassing themselves in front of others when speaking. However, it is generally believed that children and teenagers between the ages of 3 and 18 can learn a new language equally well.

Even before you leave, you should therefore take some time to prepare your children for the upcoming move. Depending on the age of the children, you can watch Spanish movies or children's series together, playfully discover the language with your children, or take language lessons.

Child benefits

Before you move to Spain, it would be helpful to know about your local financial resources and allowances. When you register your new residence in Spain, you may have to reckon with the fact that your accustomed home country's child benefit payments (if there are any) will not continue. However, there are some exceptions under which you may continue to be entitled to these monthly payments. The most crucial factor is in which country you are liable for paying taxes. I you live and work in Spain, you are therefore usually no longer entitled to your home country's social payments. It is therefore advisable to find out exactly whether your right to child benefits is forfeited by your move to Spain. You can get personal information about the payments at the family office of your local (Federal) Employment Agency.

In general, child benefits in Spain are only paid to families whose earnings are below the income limit. In plain language, this means that you are not entitled to child benefits once you earn more than € 14,000 per year. Moreover, the child benefits are also significantly lower than comparable payments in the US and UK. The payments in Spain now amount for up to € 115 per child per month after having been raised significantly in 2023. However, there is an exception for working mothers with small children. They can apply to the Agencia Tributaria for a monthly allowance of € 100 for each child under the age of three. Other subsidies are paid to large families or parents of children with disabilities[46].

School and kindergarten

If you plan to move with your children, be sure to look for a local school. Depending on your location inside the country, there are various options. In big cities, you usually even have the option of sending your children to an international English-speaking school. Ideally, you should register your children in their new school about three months before moving to Spain.

You should also be aware that in some areas of the country (e.g., Catalonia, Valencia, and the Basque Country), other languages are spoken and taught in addition to Spanish.

To make it easier for your children to get started in Spain, you might want to familiarize them beforehand with the Spanish language they will be taught locally. Of course, you should also remember to deregister your children from your home country's school in good time. In any case, you can learn more about the Spanish school system and school search later in this book.

Moving to Spain with pets

Spain is a great place to be a pet owner. Maybe you have even heard about a new law introduced in the country in 2021 giving pets more rights, e.g., in the event a couple who own a pet breakup. Moreover, there are many vets practicing in Spain looking after your beloved pet. In areas with many expats, you can often even find vets who speak English. However, some customs regarding pets might be a little bit different in your country. Before moving, you might want to know that dogs are generally banned on most beaches in Spain. During high season they are even officially prohibited from entering the beaches. There are usually specific dog beaches that you and your furry friend can visit instead. Also, many restaurants and shops don't permit dogs inside. The same goes for many types of public transport (often pets need to be carried inside of a bag) and public buildings. So, make sure to check the requirements before entering.

In the following section, we just assume that your pet belongs to the category "Cats, dogs, and ferrets entering from a non-EU country for non-commercial purposes." If your pet doesn't belong to this category, you can check the further links for information on other types of animals[47]. In the following, we also assume that you will enter the EU with your animal through Spain. If you are entering from or to another EU country first, make sure to check the requirement of that country (transits don't count as long as you don't leave the airport). When entering the EU with your pet, the first crucial thing to know is that you or a designated person issued in your pet's papers should accompany your pet at all times during the trip. If your pet travels alone (traveling alone is meant in a "being sent via a carrier" kind of way and not in a traveling alone like Garfield would kind of way which honestly would be way more impressive) or with someone else, other rules might apply. If your pet will be transported by different means of transport than you, make sure to schedule its transport within five days of your own moving day. Otherwise, the transport might fall under the category of commercial transportation.

I highly recommend you have your vet assist you with the preparations. For this, it's advisable to get in touch at least three months before your moving date. I'd recommend scheduling your first appointment even earlier than that.

Besides traveling within five days from you, some more requirements have to be fulfilled if you want to enter Spain with your pet from a non-EU country. The most important one is that your pet is microchipped. In the ideal case, the microchip your pet is wearing is ISO compliant (11784 and 11785). If your fluffy friend has a microchip that is not ISO compliant, in some cases, there is an option to carry your own microchip reader with you during the trip. Check with your vet about the different options. If your pet got a tattoo before 03rd July 2011, it will also be accepted instead of a microchip. Another critical factor is that your animal must have a valid rabies vaccine. It's crucial that your pet must already be microchipped to confirm its identity at the point of vaccination. Moreover, the vaccine must be properly documented by a vet. If the pet has not been microchipped before or the vaccine proof is not properly documented, the vaccine must be repeated. Your pet has to get the rabies shot at least 21 days before the travel date. In order to meet these requirements, your animal must be at least 15 weeks old as per EU regulations, the animal must be at least 12 weeks old when getting its rabies vaccine. If you enter from a non-Annex II regulations country, the minimum age is seven months. If you travel from a country that doesn't belong to Annex II Regulations 577/2013[48] (but don't worry, the United States, UK, Australia, and Canada do belong to them), you will need an additional serological test for rabies in an approved laboratory if you want to enter the EU with your animal. Those who want to travel with their animal in Europe are obligated to carry an EU passport for their animal. If you are from the UK and have an EU passport that was issued in Great Britain, note that the passport is not valid anymore because of Brexit. However, if your pet's EU passport was issued in another EU country, you can still use it for traveling with your pet. If you don't have an EU-issued animal passport, you will need official proof of vaccination and a health certificate, which is called an animal health certificate (AHC)[49] signed by a vet from your country, including its translation to Spanish. The AHC should not be older than ten days on the day of your EU entry. If you are a US citizen, make sure to visit a vet who is USDA certified[50]. Besides the AHC, another health certificate, the Export Health Certificate, in short EHC, must be carried with you. Check your airline requirements as you might have to provide this document when checking in with your pet. When you have all your documents in place, the last necessary regulation is that you can only enter Spain through one of the designated traveler entry points[51] (which is basically most international airports and seaports) and declare to Guardia Civil's Tax Office that you are traveling with a pet. Once you arrive in Spain, you should get an official EU passport for your pet. This will allow it to travel within the EU and to some non-EU countries without having to go through the whole process again. Most licensed vets in the country are certified to issue an EU passport for your pet. However, an EU vet, aka my sister, told me that theoretically, the vets are not allowed to copy the vaccines from your pet's old vaccination card to the EU passport. This means you might have to wait to get an EU passport for your pet until the next rabies vaccine is due. To be on the safe side, you might want to bring both passports when traveling during the first years, so you have proof of the old and new vaccines at hand.

That was a lot of information to take in. So, let's summarize the whole thing. On the day of traveling to Spain, your pet:[52]

- Must be microchipped with an ISO compliant (11784 and 11785) chip (or have a tattoo done before 03rd July 2011)
- Have a valid rabies vaccination for at least 21 days (and must have been microchipped before receiving the vaccine)
- Must be at least 15 weeks old
- Have a valid animal health certificate (AHC) signed by a vet not older than ten days
- Have a valid Export Health Certificate (EHC)
- Always be accompanied by its owner or designated traveler during the trip
- Must travel with or within five days from its owner
- Must enter Spain at one of the designated Traveler Entry Points

Transportation of your pet to Spain

If you have never traveled to the EU with your pet before, transportation can be a big planning point and a significant stress factor for your trip. The good news is that most airlines allow you to travel with your pet. In order to do so, you will have to book an extra ticket for each of the animals traveling with you. They are usually reasonably cheaper than tickets for humans, though. All airlines are free to have their own rules regarding traveling with animals, so make sure to check the airline's specific regulations before purchasing your ticket. Most airlines allow dogs and cats up to 8 kg/20 lb. to travel with their owners in the cabin. Bigger animals will usually have to be transported in their cages in an air-conditioned part of the hold. In any case, since many airlines will allow only a limited number of pets per cabin, you might want to make sure to book your ticket well in advance. In general, the pet must stay inside its box or bag during the whole duration of the flight. Usually, the only exceptions of these rules are Emotional Support Animals (*ESA*). If your dog is well-trained and you meet specific criteria (e.g., a certification from a psychiatrist), you can register your pet as an ESA before your flight. Check whether your dog can meet the criteria with your vet or licensed dog trainer. It's important to check whether your airline has regulations for the type of bag you transport your animal in. Most airlines demand that the bag fits under the seat in front of you. So, make sure to check the required bag's maximum sizes of your airline before purchasing a travel bag for your pet. There can also be other criteria your pet's travel bag need to meet, such as a waterproof bottom part or similar. If you bring your animal with you to the cabin, it will be expected to stay quiet during the entire flight and not disturb other passengers. If you are not sure your animal will remain calm, you might want to check with your dog trainer or vet for specific training or even medication to keep your pet relaxed and calm during the flight. Before boarding the aircraft, check where the pet relief areas are at the station so your dog can relieve itself before the flight.

3 months before moving up to your moving day

Applying for your Spanish visa

Now that you have decided which visa to apply for in an earlier step, it's finally time to apply for your visa. It's essential that you check when and how to apply for your visa early on, so you won't have any trouble entering the country once your moving day has arrived.

How and where to apply for your visa

When applying for a visa, your nearest Spanish embassy or consulate is responsible for you. Google the nearest Spanish embassy or consulate and make an appointment through their website or phone. I recommend you check for an appointment well in advance to avoid long waiting times. Make sure to check the process duration and waiting times on their website in order to know when you should apply for your visa.

Moreover, each embassy or consulate has all the information you need to apply for your visa presented on their website, which also includes information on the required documents and where to get them. You might want to get in touch with them anyway before submitting your documents asking for specific requirements for your case. They can help you choose the best appropriate visa for you personally and assist you with the needed documents.

Visa cost

Depending on your nationality and in which country you apply for your visa, the prices might differ. Other factors that can influence the price of your visa are your age and the age of your children (younger children are sometimes free of charge) or the type of visa you are applying for. In the following table, you can get an idea of the different visa prices. The prices don't include an additional emigration fee or residency permit fee that some consulates might charge. Moreover, the cost may differ between the consulates and are just presented here for a general overview.

	Non-Lucrative Visa	Visa for Employees	Visa for Self-Employed
USA[53]	$ 140	$ 190	$ 486
UK[54]	£ 516	£ 409	£ 966
Canada[55]	CAD 762	CAD 150	CAD 1,012
Australia	AUD 98	AUD 126	AUD 126

Visa requirements and application documents

Each of the different visa types comes with its own specific visa requirements and mandatory documents. In the following part, you will find an overview of the particular requirements for each visa. But first, let's talk quickly about the documents that are required for most visa types and where to get them. Make sure to also check whether there are specific timeframes for the age of your documents as some of the documents might only be valid for a couple of weeks. In general, it should certainly be enough if you start collecting your documents about one and a half months up to one month before your visa application appointment.

First of all, you will need your passport. If you don't have one yet, make sure to apply for one well in advance, as it can take up to some weeks to process a new passport. If you already have a passport, make sure that it has not expired yet and is not going to expire for at least six more months. If your passport is going to expire in the near future, you might want to think about applying for a new one, so you don't have to be bothered with applying for a new one in the embassy of your country right after arriving in Spain. Some embassies even require that your passport does not expire for the length of the visa you are applying for. Once you have a valid passport, make a copy of the most important pages. You should also make sure that there are at least two blank pages inside your passport, on which your visa can be issued, and your entry can be stamped. Besides your passport, you might need to bring one or two pictures of you in Spanish passport format which is usually 32 x 26 mm (1.25 x 1 in). The photos should follow the general international standard for passport pictures, such as facing the camera, nothing covering your face, white background, etc.

For most visas that include work permits, you will need a job contract or a binding job invitation letter, while for visas not including work permits, you will need to prove sufficient funds in your name to finance your life in the country for the time of your stay. The requested funds are based on what is called the *IPREM*. The IPREM determines the minimal annual income per person in Spain. If you want to become a resident without a work permit, you will have to prove that you currently own at least 400 % of the ongoing IPREM. For each of your dependents, you will need to add another annual amount of the IPREM. For 2023, the yearly IPREM equals € 7,200[56]. Based on this, you will need to prove at least € 28,800 to your name. For each dependent (like your spouse, child, or dependent parent), you will need to add another € 7,200. Another option to prove sufficient funds can be confirmation of a (passive) monthly income of at least € 2,400 (+ an additional € 600 per dependent). Such proof could be a pension plan, a remote work contract, or other types of regular (passive) income streams, like rent or dividends. To make sure that the money is actually yours, the processing consulate might ask for your bank statements up to six to 12 months before the application date. It's usually no problem if the whole amount is divided between different bank accounts. The only important thing is that they are in your name.

Another document they will definitely ask you to provide when applying for a visa to Spain is the lack of a criminal record. You will have to get the document from the country you are currently living in. While the procedure might differ between the countries, in general, it's fairly easy to get. If you are applying from the US, you will have to request what is called the *Certificate of good conduct* or *lack of criminal record*. You can request such a document with the FBI within around five business days. Find the official guide on how to do so in the further links[57]. If you have lived in the same state for the past five years, a certificate from your State Justice Department will usually do the trick. If you are a UK citizen, you can apply at the ACRO[58], the criminal records office. Apply on their website and receive your document within 12 business days (or four if you pay extra). While some US states might be able to provide the documents in Spanish, in most cases, you will need to get your document translated by an official (sworn) translator. You can find such translators on the website of your nearest consulate or simply by googling it. In most cases, your criminal record certificate will only be accepted if it's authorized with the Hague Apostille. This is an authorization certifying official documents being issued in other countries as part of the Hague 1961 convention treaty. If your documents need to be certified by the Hague Apostille (which most consulates will ask you to), you can get in touch with the Bureau of Consular Affairs[59] if you are a US citizen. As a UK citizen, you should contact the *Legalisation office*[60]. In any case, it's vital that the document you send to be legalized is the original document. Note that it might take several weeks to be processed if you do the legalization by post. Most consulates will ask you to provide the documents in Spanish.

Besides providing evidence that you don't have a criminal record, you will also need to deliver a declaration of good health. Generally, an official certified medical doctor will be able to provide such a document. Many consulates provide a template on their website that your doctor simply needs to fill out. This paper is needed to prove that you are in good physical and mental health. The easiest way is to make your doctor sign a bilingual document in English and Spanish. Otherwise, you will most likely have to get the certificate translated before handing it in.

For most visa options, you will also need to provide

proof of health insurance for your stay in the country. Although some consulates might allow health insurance from your country of residence to cover you for your stay abroad, most will obligate you to take out private Spanish insurance. By googling for options, you can decide between different providers. Depending on your age and medical history, you will prefer one or the other, which is why I am not recommending any at this point. Finding a Spanish insurance provider is usually relatively easy as many of them have their information in English. The insurance providers are used to the procedures and often offer insurance packages that specifically meet expats' needs. Besides being issued by a Spanish provider, your insurance shouldn't come with any type of copayment. Often the process of taking out Spanish medical insurance only takes a couple of working days. Make sure to print and copy the official insurance contract and payment confirmation, such as a list of everything included in your insurance plan. Make sure that all this information is in Spanish.

Another thing you might be asked to provide is proof of accommodation in the country. This can be a rental contract or real estate you own. If you don't currently have any accommodation confirmed yet, you can write a letter explaining why you chose a certain city or region to stay. Check with your local consulate about what information exactly has to be provided and how such a letter should look.

One last thing to check off before your visa application date is the payment of your visa fees. For this, you can check with your local authorities about the most recent visa fees and the accepted payment methods.

A little tip at this point: You might want to gather all the needed documents in good time and send all of them together to a sworn translator. It will be easier and faster than sending each document separately. If you do this early enough, you won't get stressed if the translators you contact don't have any free spots at the moment and you have to wait a couple of days for your documents to be translated to Spanish. If you are from a state or area where there are many Spanish speakers, you can ask directly whether certificates could be issued in Spanish. This could save you some time and money for translations. You could do so e.g., for your certificate of good health or your bank statement for proof of sufficient funds.

Ensure you check with your local authorities before submitting the documents about any local peculiarities, exceptions, or changes in the procedure. The process can differ between countries, and personal conditions can lead to the necessity of additional documents or procedures. The following requirements for each of the four most popular types of visas are meant for you to get a general overview of what is needed from your side. Depending on your case, you might need to hand in additional papers like a letter of intent, marriage or birth certificates. Also, you can never bring enough documents. So, make copies of every single one of your documents just to be sure.

Non-lucrative visa

- The National Visa application form (can be found on the website of your nearest Spanish embassy or consulate)
- Your passport (still valid for at least six more months, with at least two blank pages)
- Proof of sufficient financial funds (proof of bank account to your name with at least € 28,800 on it + € 7,200 more for each dependent joining your visa) or proof of monthly income of at least € 2,400 (+ an additional € 600 per dependent). When renewing your visa, you will be asked to prove double this

amount as your visa will be valid for two years.

- Passport-type photo
- Proof of private medical insurance covering you in Spain (most consulates ask specifically for a Spanish insurance company without any form of copayment)
- Proof of accommodation (if you already have one – which could be a lease agreement, a rental contract, or similar)
- Proof that you have no police record in your home country, e.g., Federal or State Police Record (certified with the Hague Apostille)
- Certificate of Good Health/Medical Certificate provided by an official source proving that you are in good physical and mental health (some consulates in the US and UK provide a template that your doctor can fill out)
- If you bring dependents, you will need a marriage certificate for your spouse and birth certificates for each of your children (certified with the Hague Apostille)
- Payment of the visa fee
- Note that some authorities ask for an official Spanish translation for each of the documents, so make sure to check with your local authorities before submitting your documents

Employment visa

- The National Visa application form (can be found on the website of your nearest Spanish embassy or consulate)
- Your passport (still valid for at least six more months) + copy
- Passport-type photo
- Work contract or invitation letter from your future employer (original and copy)

- Authorization of Spanish work and residence permit approval (*"comunicación de autorización de trabajo y residencia"*) issued by the Oficina Extranjeros o Dirección General de Inmigración of the Ministerio de Trabajo e Inmigración not older than 30 days (to be requested and provided by your employer)
- Proof of accommodation (if you already have one – which could be a lease agreement, a rental contract, or similar)
- Proof that you have no police record, e.g., Federal or State Police Record (certified with the Hague Apostille)
- Certificate of Good Health/Medical Certificate provided by an official source proving that you are in good physical and mental health (most consulates in the US and UK provide a template that your doctor can fill out)
- Payment of the visa fee
- Note that some authorities ask for an official Spanish translation for each of the documents, so make sure to check with your local authorities before submitting your documents

Self-employment visa

- The National Visa application form (can be found on the website of your nearest Spanish embassy or consulate)[61]
- Your passport (still valid for at least six more months) + copy
- Passport-type photo
- EX 07 Form[62]
- Modelo 790-52 Form[63]
- Modelo 790-62 Form[64]
- Business plan for the activities you plan to carry out

in Spain, including financial aspects and the number of jobs you are planning to create
- Copy of documents proving the professional training needed to carry out your planned activities in Spain
- Proof of sufficient funds, which can be own income, loans, or investments
- Other important documents such as a building lease, work permits, or similar
- Proof of accommodation (if you already have one – which could be a lease agreement, a rental contract, or similar)
- Proof that you don't have a police record, e.g., Federal or State Police Record (certified with the Hague Apostille)
- Certificate of Good Health/Medical Certificate provided by an official source proving that you are in good physical and mental health (most consulates in the US and UK provide a template that your doctor can fill out)
- Payment of the Visa Fee
- UPTA certificate[65]
- Note that some authorities ask for an official Spanish translation for each of the documents, so make sure to check with your local authorities before submitting your documents

Digital Nomad visa

- The National Visa application form (can be found on the website of your nearest Spanish embassy or consulate)
- Your passport (still valid for at least six more months, with at least two blank pages)
- Proof of sufficient financial funds (proof of bank account to your name with at least € 25,000 and

€ 9,441 more for each dependent joining your visa) or proof of sufficient monthly income
- Proof of employment or regular income + income tax return
- Two passport-type photos
- Proof of private medical insurance covering you in Spain (most consulates ask specifically for a Spanish insurance company without any form of copayment)
- Proof of accommodation (if you already have one – which could be a lease agreement, a rental contract, or similar) or travel itinerary
- Proof that you have no police record in your home country, e.g., Federal or State Police Record (certified with the Hague Apostille)
- If you bring dependents, you will need a marriage certificate for your spouse and birth certificates for each of your children (certified with the Hague Apostille)
- Payment of the visa fee (around € 80)
- Note that some authorities ask for an official Spanish translation for each of the documents, so make sure to check with your local authorities before submitting your documents

Student visa

- The National Visa application form (can be found on the website of your nearest Spanish embassy or consulate)
- Your passport (still valid for at least six more months) + copy
- Passport-type photo
- Admission letter from your university or school with specific start and finish dates and an official seal, stamp, or signature

- Or in the case of a student exchange, voluntary work, or unpaid-internship corresponding documents issued by the institution of acceptance with specific start and finish dates and an official seal, stamp, or signature
- Proof of sufficient funds – this can change depending on the consulate you are applying from
- Proof that you don't have a police record, e.g., Federal or State Police Record (certified with the Hague Apostille)
- Certificate of Good Health/Medical Certificate provided by an official source proving that you are in good physical and mental health (most consulates in the US and UK provide a template that your doctor can fill out)
- Proof of health insurance covering you during your entire stay in Spain (without any kind of copayment)
- Payment of the visa fee
- If the applicant is under 18 years of age: a notarized authorization letter from parents or legal guardian + information and sworn declaration of the host family
- Note that some authorities ask for an official Spanish translation for each of the documents, so make sure to check with your local authorities before submitting your documents

Visa pickup

Once your visa is issued, you will be notified per email. Depending on the option you have chosen, you can either pick it up at the embassy or consulate it was issued in or it will be sent to you by mail. Either way, you usually now have 90 days counted from the visa approval date to enter Spain.

Cancel or take out last insurances

Now, at the latest, it is time to cancel the last insurance if you haven't already done that. This includes all insurances that don't offer protection when you no longer have a residence in your country.

It may take a few weeks until you have registered with the Spanish health care system. You should therefore make sure that your insurance coverage is always guaranteed. One possibility is to keep your insurance (if insurance is covering abroad as well) for the time being. However, it is critical to determine whether your insurance coverage for Spain will continue in case of an emergency, even if you have already deregistered your residence in your country. As soon as you receive your temporary insurance card in Spain, you can cancel your old insurance.

Another option is to take out international health insurance for the first few months in your new home country.

Possibly already apply for your NIE at the local Spanish consulate

Theoretically, it is possible to apply for an NIE (*Número de Identifación de Extranjero*) before leaving for Spain. You will learn what exactly an NIE is and what you need it for later in this book.

In most cases, your NIE will automatically be issued when you receive your visa. If that's the case, no further action is needed from your side regarding your NIE. If you have an EU passport and thus no visa, I recommend you try to apply for your NIE before leaving for Spain. It's usually much easier to do so from a Spanish embassy in a foreign country than from inside of Spain. However, some consulates do not issue an NIE if the applicant plans to live in Spain for more than three months.

Obtaining the NIE through the consulate general or embassy is reserved for those who need to carry out administrative procedures in Spain, such as buying real estate or inheritance matters, without living there themselves.

You should therefore find out beforehand if you can obtain the NIE at your local consulate. If this is not possible, do not worry. The chaotic application process from Spain is somehow part of the typical expat experience.

Sale of all things that cannot be taken with you

Moving is the perfect opportunity to finally get rid of all those things you haven't used in ages anyway: old cables you no longer know which device they even belong to, vacation souvenirs gathering dust in boxes under the bed, bad buys, or half-broken items that you simply didn't want to part with until now. Because when moving, the less you take with you, the lower your moving costs will be.

Of course, this process will be more straightforward if you only want to move to Spain for a few months and return home at some point. In this case, you can store your belongings with friends or rent a storage room, garage, or similar.

But if you plan to pack all your possessions and grow old in Spain, you should think carefully about which furniture and items you really want to take with you. In fact, you can often save a lot by selling your furniture on eBay or other flea market apps and then buying new furniture locally or renting an already furnished apartment.

Organize accommodation (for the first few days) in Spain

When you arrive in Spain with all your belongings, you don't want to start looking for accommodation on the spot. You should therefore start looking for a suitable place to stay now at the latest.

Ideally, you have time to spend a few days in Spain before your move to look at suitable apartments. Especially if you want to buy a property, you should have seen it in person before making your decision. That way you can move right into your new home when you arrive in Spain.

Tip: Do not sign a contract until you have seen the property. It does not matter if it is a rental or purchase contract. If you can't see it for yourself, you can also send someone you trust to share some photos of the interior with you.

However, it is more likely that you do not have time to travel to Spain already before your move and find suitable accommodation. In this case, it may be difficult to find an apartment before you arrive. You should therefore rent accommodation for the first few days via booking platforms like Booking.com or Airbnb. Especially in big cities like Barcelona, rooms and apartments are quickly allocated. It is therefore not unrealistic that you can move into your new home within a few days.

Medications and health check

Before you leave, you might want to have a thorough medical check-up. This will give you time to apply for your health insurance card in Spain (as it may take some time). If you are dependent on regular medication, make sure to get enough of it before you leave. If possible, it is best to build up a small stockpile that will keep you afloat for a few months and protect you in case the registration process takes a little longer than initially planned.

Deregister residence in your country

Before finally heading to the south of Europe, you must deregister your residence in your country. Deregistering your residence is not only practical for you but also required by law. Moreover, especially for US citizens, it is vital to deregister in the state you currently reside in. Otherwise, you might still be charged state taxes even though you live abroad. Some states, such as California, might even keep charging you state taxes if you are still a partial-year resident (even for the time spent abroad) or keep working remotely for a state-based company. If you are a UK citizen and properly deregistered, you will most likely lose your tax resident status in the UK and only be obliged to pay taxes in Spain from now on. Exceptions are UK citizens who still have income from their country or own property there.

As a rule, deregistration should be done before your departure. All you have to do is go to the registration office of your municipality. If you are a UK citizen, you will have to deregister with your local council. In the links at the end, you can find a website that helps you find out which your local council is.[66] Make sure that they will give you a deregistration certificate. You should keep this in a safe place. If you already have a new address in Spain, you can also leave your address with the authorities. This will enable you to receive your voting documents at the next election, as you are still entitled to vote as a UK citizen and benefits you might be entitled to. Moreover, inform HM Revenue & Customs about your move abroad to let them know you won't be obligated to pay taxes in the UK anymore. You can find out how to do so in the related links[67]. If you are a US citizen, search online for "deregistration [your state]" to learn how to register from the state you are currently living in. It might be advisable to get information about the process from a professional, e.g., a local lawyer.

Deregister your car

Whether you want to take your car with you or sell it, you should deregister your car if your principal residence is no longer inside the country it is currently registered in. If you regularly live in another country and visit Spain for fewer than six months, you usually do not need to deregister or re-register your vehicle.

For most non-EU citizens, it is recommendable to sell your car and buy a new one in Spain if you need one. Between transportation costs, taxes, and registration fees, you will most likely pay more than you would pay for selling your car and buying a new one in the country.

In Spain, you have about two months after official registration to register your car in the country. In some cases, you can deregister your vehicle in your country afterward, with the help of the local Embassy or Consulate in Spain. It is best to find out if your city offers this service before you leave.

Get all the documents ready to move your pet

In an earlier part of the book, we already talked about everything you need to enter Spain with your pet. As some of the documents should not be older than ten days on your moving day, make sure to get all of them ready. Check again if all the required documents are complete and whether your pet's vaccines are properly documented. Incompleteness could lead to your pet being denied entry at the border, so make sure you have not forgotten anything.

Saying goodbye to your loved ones

This task, which is often read with a smile on our moving to Spain checklist, many times turns out to be one of the toughest hurdles once the moment of departure has come. Even though you probably already have Spain fever and can't wait to call this wonderful country your new home, you should take plenty of time to say goodbye to your loved ones before you leave. Let's face it: from now on, you will only see your friends and family when you get to visit. And I speak from experience when I say that a virtual meeting via video chat services like Skype or Zoom just isn't the same. So, despite the stress of moving, spend some quality time with your loved ones. You might even want to plan a farewell party where you can see everyone again before you head to Spain.

After your arrival in Spain

After handing over the keys to your old apartment, the most exciting part of your emigration journey is about to begin: moving into a completely new life. Whether you arrive by plane or car will certainly depend on how much luggage you have to transport and where in the world you used to live. In the following section of the book, we will deal with everything you need to know in order to start your new life in Spain perfectly prepared.

Registering in Spain

Once you have arrived on a long-term visa, it's vital that you start the registration process inside the country. Depending on which visa option you choose, you usually have just around three months to register before your visa becomes invalid. If you are familiar with the TLC series 90 days fiancé, it's basically the same, except you don't have to marry someone once the 90 days are over. If that's not a great deal... So make sure to get started with the registration process right away. Some visa options might state that you must register within 30 days of arriving in the country. But don't panic if you realize that you won't make the deadline. In some places, it's nearly impossible to get an appointment that fast and Spanish authorities are aware of that.

The Spanish identity number (NIE)

I have mentioned it quite a lot before in the previous pages, but now, I will finally tell you what this mysterious NIE thing is all about. Before you can work in Spain as a foreigner, take out insurance, or buy real estate, you need a foreigner's identity number, which is called the *Número de Identifiación de Extranjero*, or NIE for short. In other words, without the NIE, you won't be able to do almost anything. The NIE is the counterpart to the Spanish NIF, *Número de Identificación Fisical*, which Spanish citizens receive with their identity card (*DNI*). Unlike some foreign ID card numbers, the Spanish NIF does not change even when their ID card is renewed. The same applies to the NIE. You most probably have received your NIE already printed on your visa. In this case, you can ignore the following process and move on to the next step. If you haven't received your NIE yet, this is the first thing you should be taking care of after arriving in the country. The NIE number never expires or changes, so it makes sense to learn it as you will be asked for it all the time, e.g., when accepting mail at your door or for bureaucratic formalities.

What is the NIE and what do we use it for?

The *Número de Identificación de Extranjero* (Identity Number for Foreigners), or NIE for short, is probably the most important piece of paper you will need for your life in Spain. You can think of it as your Spanish fingerprint. You will need the NIE if you:

- want to work in Spain
- open a Spanish bank account
- want to take out contracts (e.g., Internet, gas, water, or mobile telephone)

- study in Spain
- buy property
- vote in the mayoral elections
- and for almost all bureaucratic matters in the country

How to apply for the NIE with a non-EU passport

Most probably, you have received your NIE already printed on your visa. If, for any reason, you haven't received your NIE yet when entering Spain, you should apply for it. You can usually just do so when registering your fingerprints (I will tell you more about that in a second). Simply print the Formular EX 15[68], fill it out accordingly and bring it with you when registering your fingerprints at the foreigner's office.

How to apply for the NIE with an EU passport

- Get an appointment (Cita Previa) online Monday morning at 8 am* - See the next section for detailed instructions.
- Bring the following documents to the appointment
  - The application document (No. 15)[69]
  - Passport and copy of passport or ID card and copy of ID card
  - Empadronamiento document
  - Employment contract, invitation from employer, enrollment certificate or bank statement with enough money on it (at least € 6,000 per person)
  - Document about the payment of the fee (No. 790[70])

- If you do not speak Spanish, it is best to take someone with you to translate - almost no one speaks English
- Check your data after receiving the documents

* At the moment, it seems to be particularly difficult to allocate an appointment. More and more companies specialize in requesting all appointments and then selling them to newly arrived emigrants for up to € 250. You should therefore try to do it on different days during the week. The latest tip is the app Cita Previa Extranjería71, which you can download for free from the Appstore. It works just like the website and informs you as soon as new dates are available.

How to get an appointment (*Cita Previa*) for the NIE

1. Open the website[72] in your browser or in the app *Cita Previa Extranjería*[73] (recommended)
2. Select your province and click on *Aceptar*
3. Select *Policia - Certificados UE*, and then click Aceptar
4. Click on *Entrar*
5. Enter your NIE, passport, or ID card number
6. Enter your name and surname
7. Select the country of your citizenship (e.g., *Alemania* for Germany)
8. Then click on *Aceptar*
9. Now click on *Solicitar Cita*
10. Now you can either choose a date or you will be informed that there are no appointments available at the moment - if that's the case, try again later

The Spanish Foreigner Identity Card (TIE) (Only for non-EU passport holders)

What is the TIE and what do we use it for?

The *Tarjeta de identidad de extranjero* (identity card for foreigners), or TIE, is an identification document required in the country by foreigners from outside the EU. Besides the NIE number, it's the most vital thing to apply for when moving to Spain. Apart from the passport from your country, it will be your most important identity document while living and traveling inside of the EU.

The TIE is a little passport, including your NIE number and your photo. Every time you are asked for your NIE number in the future, this is the document to show. Once you have received your TIE, it will be valid for your visa's duration.

What is the difference between the NIE and the TIE?

The NIE is the *Número de Identificación de Extranjero* (Identity Number for Foreigners) and is therefore required by all foreigners who wish to live in the country. The *Tarjeta de identidad de extranjero* (identity card for foreigners), or TIE, is an identification document required in the country by foreigners from outside the EU. In short, the NIE is only the number, while the TIE is a physical card that contains your NIE number. So, if you are moving to Spain from a non-EU country, you will need both the NIE and the TIE. If you have an EU passport, you won't need the TIE.

How to apply for the TIE

The first step of your NIE application process will be scanning your fingerprints. Once you have an appointment, you will also show all the necessary documents. After a waiting time of around 30 to 60 days, they will notify you that your TIE is ready for pickup. While you used to be able to simply walk to the foreigner's police office and pick it up, thanks to the pandemic, you will now need a specific appointment to do so. More on that later. While waiting for your appointment to register your fingerprints, you should already complete the next step of registering in the civil register to receive your padrón (more on this in the next step).

- Get an appointment (*Cita Previa*) online Monday morning at 8 am* - See the next section for detailed instructions

* At the moment, it seems to be particularly difficult to allocate an appointment. More and more companies specialize in requesting all appointments and then selling them to newly-arrived emigrants for up to € 250. You should therefore try to do it on different days during the week. The latest tip is the app *Cita Previa Extranjería*[74], which you can download for free from the Appstore. It works just like the website and informs you as soon as new dates are available.

How to get an appointment (*Cita Previa*) for the TIE

1. Open the website[75] in your browser or in the app *Cita Previa Extranjería*[76] (recommended)
2. Select your province and click on *Aceptar*

3. Select *Toma de Huellas*, and then click Aceptar
4. Click on *Entrar*
5. Enter your NIE, passport, or ID card number
6. Enter your name and surname
7. Select the country of your citizenship (e.g., *EEUU* (Estados Unidos) for USA)
8. Then click on *Aceptar*
9. Now click on *Solicitar Cita*
10. Now you can either choose a date or you will be informed that there are no appointments available at the moment - if that's the case, try again later
11. If you need to register the fingerprints for more than one person, make sure to get one appointment for each person

Registration in the civil register – El Padrón

After applying for an appointment to register your fingerprints for your TIE, you should already complete the registration in the local civil register. It's important to have this step completed before registering your fingerprints, as you will need to provide the document that you will receive in this step when registering your fingerprints. Anyone staying in the country for more than three months is required to register in the municipality's population register. This process is called empadronamiento. Although the name may sound rather complicated, this is in principle one of the quickest and easiest official procedures to complete. The simplicity of this task is probably mainly because the process of empadronamiento is the same for foreigners as it is for locals. As soon as you have been registered, you will receive what is called the Padrón with the Certificado de Empadronamiento. You will need this certificate for the following processes:

- Application for the health insurance card (*Tarjeta Sanitaria*)
- Application for Residencia
- Car purchase
- School registration of your children
- Marriage

As a rule, your registration certificate should not be older than four months for any of these processes. You can retrieve and print a current document at any time online or at a city vending machine.

The Empadronamiento procedure

To obtain the Certificado de Empadronamiento, you must first request an appointment at the city hall (*Ayuntamiento*) of your city. Depending on the municipality, appointments can be made online or by phone (see the links below for the websites of Barcelona[77] and Madrid[78]).

You will need the following documents in order to register:

- Passport
- Copy of your passport
- Rental contract and copy of the rental contract
- Completed document (each municipality has its own document)

If you do not have a rental contract, they will accept written confirmation from your landlord or roommate (together with a copy of the person's identity card) or a contract (electricity, water, internet) in your name and address.

Registering your fingerprints (only for Non-EU passport holders)

Once the day of your appointment that you applied for in an earlier step has come, make sure to arrive at the foreigner's office on time. It's recommended to take a screenshot from your appointment confirmation email to show the guard at the door of the foreigner's office. Make sure you have all required documents with you to present to the official while your fingerprints are being registered. Pay the TIE administration fee before your appointment by printing and filling out the document modelo 790-12. You can theoretically pay the fee in any bank and get a stamp on this paper as proof of payment. However, some banks might only let you pay the fee if you have a bank account with them. After registering your fingerprints, when everything has been checked, and the civil servant has confirmed that nothing is missing, you can go home and wait for the confirmation that your TIE has been completed. The processing time might take anywhere between 30 and 60 days. While you are waiting for your TIE to be issued, you can already proceed with the registration process. It is possible that during the waiting time, they will contact you because something is unclear to the officials, or a document might be missing. If that's the case, you will usually have to return to the foreigner's office within ten days to provide more information or missing documents. In any case, let's talk about the day of your appointment.

- Bring the following documents to the appointment:
  - The application document (No. 17[79])
  - Application form for TIE[80]

- o Passport and copy of passport (don't forget to copy the part that includes your visa as well)
- o The document about the payment of the fee (No. 790-12) (available on the website of the Spanish police[81])
- o A recent passport-sized picture of your face on a white background
- o Padrón (Empadronamiento document)
- o Your residence or working permit
- If you do not speak Spanish, it is best to take someone with you to translate - almost no one speaks English.
- While the documents just mentioned are the officially required ones, you might bring any kind of documents you have such as a work contract or similar – just in case
- Check if all data they entered is correct

TIE pickup

When your TIE has been issued and is ready for pickup, you will receive a confirmation email. Picking up your TIE is arguably the easiest part of registering in Spain. However, you will need an appointment to pick it up due to the pandemic. Some fortunate people might tell you that they went to pick it up without an appointment, but it's usually a waste of time to try. Follow the instructions below to get an appointment for the TIE pickup. On the day of your appointment, make sure you arrive on time and present the appointment confirmation (on your phone) to the guard at the door.

How to get an appointment (*Cita Previa*) for the TIE pickup

1. Open the website[82] in your browser or in the app *Cita Previa Extranjería*[83] (recommended)
2. Select your province and click on *Aceptar*
3. Make sure to select the same office you went to when you registered your fingerprints under the dropdown menu *Oficina*
4. Select *Recogida de Tarjeta Identidad de Extranjero (TIE)*, and then click *Aceptar*
5. Click on *Entrar*
6. Enter your NIE, passport, or ID card number
7. Enter your name and surname
8. Select the country of your citizenship (e.g., *EEUU* (Estados Unidos) for USA)
9. Then click on *Aceptar*
10. Now click on *Solicitar Cita*
11. Now you can either choose an appointment or you will be informed that there are no appointments available at the moment - if that's the case, try again later
12. Once you have gotten the confirmation, take a screenshot of the appointment confirmation – just in case (you will receive an email with the confirmation, appointment time and date)

The Spanish Social Security - Seguridad Social (only for work permit holders and EU-passport holders)

Like most other EU countries, every worker in Spain is subject to social insurance. This means that you have to register with the Spanish social security, the *Seguridad Social* before you can start working in the country. This step is only necessary if you are planning to work in Spain. If you entered Spain on a non-lucrative or student visa, you therefore do not have to register with social security and can simply skip this step. Compared to applying for the NIE and the TIE, registering with Social Security is relatively easy and only takes a few hours (including waiting time). Seguridad Social combines local health and pension insurance. This means that anyone who is employed in Spain is automatically provided with health insurance. The insurance is completely free of charge for you, as the costs are covered either by the employer or by the state. To be eligible for unemployment benefits, you must have worked in Spain for at least one year and paid into the social security system.

Registering with Social Security

To register for Social Security, you generally have to show up in person. You can easily find out which Social Security office is closest to you by visiting the Seguridad Social website. This will also tell you if you need an appointment (*cita previa*) or if you simply need to draw a number when you arrive. Either way, you should bring a little time, patience, and perhaps something to pass the time. Spanish government procedures are not for the faint of heart.

You will also need the following documents to register for social security:

- Passport
- NIE (if available)
- Employment contract (if available)
- Completed registration form (will be given to you at the office and can be filled in on the spot)

As soon as you are called in, hand over your documents to the employee, and after a short wait, you will receive the original document with your new social security number. Be sure to check whether all your information is correct. In my case, my date of birth and passport number was entered incorrectly, which led to problems later on. Also, register your phone number. This will give you the option to access essential documents online in the future and save you the trip to the Social Security Office. In addition, you will receive important changes and information via SMS from now on.

Opening a Spanish bank account

What is surprising for many expats is that you need a Spanish bank account if you want to live in Spain. Most Spanish companies refuse to transfer your salary to foreign bank accounts. The same goes for many mobile phone and internet providers, where you need a Spanish account to use their services.

Many banks require a residencia (TIE) or at least an NIE to open a Spanish bank account. The banks that let you open an account without an NIE often have high banking fees. Opening an account in Spain is probably similar to opening an account in your home country and is relatively easy. First, however, you should compare the prices and services of the different banks. There is also the option of switching to online banks such as *Evo*, which are often much cheaper.

The Spanish Public Health Insurance card – Tarjeta Sanitaria (only for work permit and EU-passport holders)

First of all, you can only take advantage of the Spanish healthcare system if you are part of the Spanish

Social Security system. If you are in Spain on a non-lucrative, student visa or similar, you are thus not able to apply for the Tarjeta Sanitaria. But if you are officially registered as a resident of Spain, you can use the public health insurance. Because only after you have applied for the Spanish health insurance card should you cancel your current health or foreign insurance. As mentioned above, health insurance in Spain is free of charge for all employees. However, you must first apply for your health insurance card (*Tarjeta Sanitaria*) to access the health insurance system. With the Tarjeta Sanitaria, you will then have access to the Emergency Medical Service (*CAP Urgencias*) and public hospitals (*hospital público*). Your insurance also includes your spouse and children up to the age of 26. Medical services in Spain are considered very good. However, you should be prepared for long waiting times with specialists in Spain with statutory health insurance.

Requesting the Tarjeta Sanitaria

Depending on your municipality, you can apply for your health card at the nearest health center (*Centro de Salud*) or CAP (*Centro de Atención Primaria*). You will need the following documents to apply for your health card:

- Social security document
- NIE
- Certificado de Empadronamiento

After the paperwork has been completed, you will first receive a temporary health insurance card on paper. With this, you already have the possibility to use medical services. The actual health insurance card will be sent to you later. Like everything else, this can take several weeks to months. If you do not have a permanent address or are planning to move in the next few weeks, you should have your health insurance card sent directly to the CAP and pick it up there.

Private medical insurance in Spain

Like in most other Western countries, you have the option of taking out private health insurance in Spain in addition to your statutory health insurance. If you don't have a Spanish work permit or are registered with the Spanish Social Security, most probably you already have private health insurance. Private health insurance gives you access to private medical practices, specialists, and private hospitals. This also means that waiting times for appointments or test results are usually drastically reduced. Your chosen insurance may also include supplementary dental insurance. Private health insurance in Spain is generally much more affordable compared to many other European countries. Of course, the costs and included services differ depending on the provider, age, and pre-existing conditions. For comparison: My husband pays about € 600 per year for his private health insurance (mid-30s and without pre-existing conditions), for example.

Apartment hunting in Spain

Searching for an apartment can vary greatly depending on the city or province you choose. In big cities like Madrid or Barcelona in particular, the search is easier if you have already arrived in town. Since the number of people looking for a place to stay tends to be quite large, the apartments and rooms are usually only allocated at short notice. It is therefore often not worthwhile to start looking for an apartment in advance.

The housing market in the popular big cities,

especially Barcelona, can be tumultuous. There are always rooms and apartments rented far above their actual value. For this reason, you should never sign a rental contract without you or someone you trust having personally inspected the accommodation beforehand.

The easiest way to find available accommodation is online. On numerous platforms such as Idealista, Fotocasa, pisocompartido.com, and Badi.com, landlords can post their apartments or rooms for rent. Another way to find a suitable place to stay is through Facebook groups. Just enter "Piso en [place in Spain]" in the search option, and you will indeed find a suitable group.

How not to fall victim to a renting scam

In general, Spanish tenancy law differs from many common international tenancy laws and offers all kinds of legal loopholes that some landlords love to use. It is therefore worthwhile to be particularly careful when concluding a rental agreement and to be on the safe side. The following information refers to residential leases and not commercial or seasonal leases.

First of all, you should know that both written and oral contracts are valid. However, you should always insist on a written lease. This will not only make it easier for you to register but will also help you to be on the safe side legally. Therefore, be careful. If you don't speak Spanish or are unsure, ask a local or lawyer to look over the contract before you sign it.

Also, before you sign a contract, be sure to check for discrepancies to avoid being ripped off. One popular scam, for example, is called the key trick. Here, you are charged security payments or advance payments for apartments that have already been rented. If you have fallen for such a scam, the only option you have is to file a lawsuit. Even if the fraudsters are found, the process can take several years to be concluded. It is therefore imperative that you give importance to any discrepancy. Another helpful tip is expat forums on the Internet or Facebook groups, where you can find out about the latest scams and exchange information with other emigrants.

In addition, you should check the functionality of all appliances in the house (e.g., kitchen appliances, faucets, heating, etc.) before signing the contract. Spanish rental law does not provide for a rent reduction in the event of defects in the apartment[84].

The Spanish rental contract

Once you've found a suitable place to live, it's time to sign the rental contract. A regular lease generally runs for five years. However, if your landlord is a company, the standard contract term is as long as seven years. In this case, both parties have an extraordinary right of termination in the event of non-compliance with the lease agreement. For you as a tenant, a minimum contract term of six months applies. This means that you have an ordinary right of termination after this period. If stipulated in the contract, you may be subject to "penalty payments" of a maximum of one month's rent per year if you terminate the contract earlier. In addition, you should pay attention to the length of the notice period, which should also be specified in the lease agreement.

Another aspect that might be interesting for you is the right of inspection. This means that the landlord is allowed to "inspect things" in the house at any time. If you disagree with this, you should have the right of inspection deleted from the contract before signing it.

The security deposit (*fianza*) is set by law in the Spanish Rental Law (*Ley de Arrendamientos Urbanos*) and is exactly one month's rent. The landlord is obligated to deposit the fianza with the appropriate office after the contract is signed and give you, the tenant, a copy of the deposit form. In addition, the landlord has the right to demand another monetary rental security from you in the form of cash. The amount of this security should also be specified in the lease agreement and should not exceed two months' rent. However, it is not uncommon for a rental deposit to be required in the amount of up to six months' rent. This is because some landlords use this money and find a reason to withhold the security payment at the end of the lease. You should therefore try to avoid leaving more than two months' rent as security.

Acquiring property

Maybe you aren't planning to rent an apartment at all but buy a property right away. Similar to the Spanish rental contract, purchasing a property in Spain is regulated somewhat differently than in many other countries. Before purchasing a property in the country, you first need an NIE. If you are not yet living in Spain, you can apply for your NIE through a Spanish embassy or consulate. After your NIE is issued, you should also open a Spanish bank account. Since the payment for a property is usually made in the form of a bank check, you should have a Spanish bank account at the latest at the time of payment.

You can either search for a suitable property yourself or use the services of an (English-speaking) real estate agent. The service of a real estate agent can provide security against fraud attempts and simplify purchasing a house. On the other hand, the services of a real estate agent incur additional costs. In any case, however, you should definitely consult an (English-speaking) Gestor or lawyer who is familiar with real estate law. In Spain, the buyer is liable for any fees that are attached to the property. Such fees can be, e.g., missing building permits. If only a notary is consulted, possible debts or special conditions with which the chosen property could be occupied are not checked. Despite everything, an additional notarization of the purchase is important to register your real estate purchase in the Spanish land register.

Furthermore, it is essential that you (or at least a person you trust) have personally viewed the property before signing a purchase contract. You can find more tips on buying real estate in Spain in the related links[85].

Annual real estate costs in Spain

In addition to the one-time purchase price, you should also be aware of the ongoing annual costs of your property. These costs are not only possible repairs and maintenance that your property may require from time to time but above all the following costs[86]:

- Taxes
- Insurance
- Incidental expenses
- Possible mortgages
- Possible community charges
- Possible community fees

Taxes can be divided into the local property tax IBI (*Impuesto sobre Buenes Inmuebles*) and state taxes. The latter is mainly based on whether you rent out your property when not in use.

Of course, if you own a property, you should also be on the safe side and take out an insurance policy that can save you from expensive surprises. For the price of your insurance, you should calculate about 0.05 % of the property price.

The utilities of your property, such as water and electricity, are calculated based on the use of the space, in addition to some possible fixed costs. Another cost factor could be a mortgage (*hipoteca*). This is calculated based on the layout and features of your property. This could be, for example, a garden or pool. The community costs (*Gastos de Comunidad*) are also calculated according to the construction and equipment. These are due if your property is located in a residential complex. For example, an existing pool or an elevator could be decisive. In addition, some municipalities charge annual community fees (*Tasas Comunales*) for garbage and sewage. In general, your yearly costs will depend greatly on the size, amenities, use, and, most importantly, the value and location of your property. It is highly recommended to find out the exact ongoing costs before buying the property.

Real estate taxes as a non-resident

If you spend less than 183 days a year in Spain, you are not considered a resident of the country for tax purposes. As a non-resident property owner, you are obliged to pay the annual non-resident tax Modelo 210 (*Impuesto sobre la Renta de no Residentes*). We have already talked about this type of tax in an earlier part of this book. The non-resident tax rate is currently 19 % for EU citizens and 24 % for non-EU citizens but fluctuates periodically. Depending on the value of your property, you should expect the approximately average cost to be between € 200 and € 600 per year.

However, you must file the information per quarter if you rent out your property. In addition, even as a non-resident, the property tax (*IBI*) must be paid.

Job hunting in Spain

If you enter Spain on an EU Blue card or work visa,

you most probably already have a permanent job when you move to Spain. This could be a transfer from your previous company to Spain or a firm job commitment that you are ready to start once you arrive in Spain. If this is the case, you can simply skip this book section. Some expats decide to enter Spain on a non-lucrative visa and look for a job on-site. Once you have been accepted and offered a position as an employee, it is vital to apply for your work permit before you start working. However, you may also be self-employed. In this case, the section under the heading *Autónomo* will help you register your activities in Spain.

As relaxed as life under the Spanish sun may be, it is unfortunately impossible to live off fresh air alone. If you cannot live from savings or pensions, bring your previous gainful employment to Spain and do not plan to become self-employed locally, you should start looking for a suitable job after arriving in the country at the latest. Many expats arrive in Spain on a non-lucrative visa and start looking for a job once they have made themselves feel comfortable. In the previous part of this book, we already talked about the recognition of your professional training in Spain. If you want to apply for one of these professions, you will need the required documents for the recognition of your professional training at the latest now.

With an average unemployment rate of 13.1 % (as of December 2022), finding a job in the country can be difficult in general. However, it all depends on what field you want to work in, where you live, and your salary expectations. Additional factors for the success of your job search can be previous work experience, education, and language skills. Overall, it is easier to get a foothold in large cities like Barcelona, Seville, and Madrid.

Generally, workers with a background in technical professions, IT, healthcare, sales, and gastronomy have good job opportunities. Typical "*foreigner jobs*" are also prevalent. Such jobs are characterized by the fact that usually no knowledge of Spanish is required. Instead, you work in English or another native language you might have. Outside of times of crisis or the pandemic, it is quite easy to get such a job in many places in Spain. However, these jobs are often poorly paid and offer little job security. Popular jobs for foreigners can be call center jobs such as sales and customer service, language teachers for popular languages or English, waiters, hotel receptionists, or babysitters. You can also consider these types of jobs as an ideal way to start your new life. Since these companies specialize in foreigners, they can help you with your TIE and other documents. In addition, you have the practical opportunity to meet new people on-site, get a first insight into Spanish working life, and increase your household budget. This way, you don't have to use up all your savings just after arriving in the country. Besides, you can always look for a more suitable job.

For many positions in the country, knowledge of Spanish or the local language (e.g., Catalan in Catalonia) is a prerequisite. If that's not another reason to learn the local language! However, since you cannot learn such a language overnight, you can also consider a Spanish job an optimal opportunity to improve your language skills if you already know the basics. So don't be discouraged from applying for a job if your Spanish isn't perfect yet. You will see that your language problems will resolve within a few weeks.

Many job postings in the country are posted on job platforms. The most popular platforms include Infojobs.net and Indeed. However, there are also many other platforms where jobs are posted (e.g., jobtoday.com or milanuncios). Just type "*Trabajo en [your city/region]*" into Google. Simply create a profile on the respective site and upload your resume. You can apply to the job postings you want with just a few clicks.

The career network LinkedIn can also be a handy way to find job postings and make professional contacts. Another common way to discover job openings is Facebook. To do so, join a regional Facebook group for expats or job seekers because job offers are regularly shared here as well.

Of course, there is also the possibility of a traditional direct application in Spain. To do this, check with the company of your choice whether they currently advertise vacancies or need personnel. You can find out, for example, on the company website or by telephone. You can then apply directly to the company. Sometimes it may also be helpful to get your first foot in the door by doing an internship at your desired company.

The application process can take weeks, depending on the job. It is therefore important that you have sufficient financial resources to tide you over for several months, if necessary, until you find a suitable job.

The Spanish employment contract

After you have completed the nerve-racking application process and finally received a job offer, an employment contract is concluded before you start work. In Spain, such a contract can be concluded in writing or verbally. However, to be on the safe side legally, you should insist on a written one. Furthermore, you will need the contract to apply for a work permit. After concluding a written agreement, you are also entitled to a copy of it, to which you should also lay claim.

Generally, there are two types of employment contracts: a fixed-term employment contract (*contrato de obra o servicio determinado*) and an indefinite employment contract (*contrato indefinido*). In addition, the contract should include the following points[87]:

- Data of employee and employer
- Start of employment
- Salary category or occupational group
- Working hours
- Starting base salary
- Date and type of salary payments
- Vacation days (note that in Spain "natural days" are often used, which include weekends)
- Notice period
- Collective agreement
- Probationary

The probationary period is not regulated by law in Spain and should therefore be specified in the employment contract. Usually, it ranges from 15 days to six months. The employment law of each employee differs according to the degree of employment specified in the employment contract: regular employee (*Trabajador*), executive employee (*Alto Directivo*), or managing director (*Administrador*). This division mainly affects protection against dismissal and the right to receive severance pay. Regardless of the type of employment, your employer must register you with Social Security after you start working for the company. This is the only way you can claim your entitlement to statutory health insurance and, in the event of dismissal, unemployment benefits. If you are unsure about your employment contract, you should consult a professional, such as a lawyer.

Contract termination and unemployment benefits

Unfortunately, in a country with such a high unemployment rate, it can happen all too quickly that you are suddenly handed a notice of termination from one day to the next. Those who rely on typical jobs for foreigners in particular are often surprised by unemployment.

Here's a little anecdote from my first job in Barcelona. After spending the first few months in Spain exclusively writing my bachelor thesis, I needed a job as soon as possible to not sacrifice all my savings right after arriving in the country. So I decided to take the first job I could get - a business development position in a French company. The project I was working on was for a well-known French e-marketplace. After barely two months at the company, my colleagues and I were already holding a spontaneous resignation in our hands for the first time. The termination came in due time 14 days before the company vacation over Christmas. This way, the French client we were working for avoided having to pay us a vacation bonus. And then, right on time at the beginning of January, I received a new contract for the same client. Since the company's location was ideal for me and the working hours gave me enough time to learn Spanish after work, I decided to give the company a second chance. But if you now think that they could not top the audacity of the last dismissal, you are wrong. Not even a quarter of a year later, we received another notice of termination. Over the weekend, all our login data had already been changed, so that on Monday morning, we initially still believed it was a technical error when none of us could log into our work platform. After about half an hour the head of the company called us in to his office to give us the "good news" that our client had spontaneously run out of the financial resources that had been approved for our project over the weekend. (We are talking about one of the 100 best earning companies in France). And so, the project was spontaneously closed. Since the project for which we had been hired no longer existed, our employer could then just throw us out without notice.

Entitlement to unemployment benefits

In general, it is essential to know that the entitlement to unemployment benefits in Spain is regulated differently from in many other European countries. In Spain, only those who have worked in the country for at least twelve months and have therefore paid into the social security system (*Seguridad Social*) are entitled to unemployment benefits (*Paro*). In addition, you are only authorized to receive unemployment benefits if you have been dismissed by your employer (however, there may be some exceptions during pandemic periods).

The duration of social benefits depends on the number of days you have previously worked. For example, you are entitled to 120 days of help if you have worked for at least one year. The amount of benefits payable is calculated based on your average salary from your last pay period. As a rule, you receive 70 % of it. The minimum amount is € 560 - for parents € 749. If you receive *paro* for a longer period of time, the payments might be reduced to 50 % later (from 180 days on) - the maximum amount is € 1,225 per month for childless persons, € 1,400 per month for parents of one child, and € 1,575 per month for parents of two or more children[88].

Autónomo – being self-employed in Spain

Of course, in addition to working as an employee, you also have the option of working in Spain as a self-employed person. Generally, you have two options: You can either start your own business or work as a freelancer, called Autónomo. If you start a business, you should register an SL. SL stands for "*Sociedad de responsabilidad Limitada*", which corresponds to LLC in the US and Ltd. in the UK.

On the other hand, you should register as an

Autónomo if you offer any kind of services. This could be, e.g., working as a language teacher, IT services, or if you work as an author or similar, like me. Make sure you check that your visa allows you to work as a freelancer in the country. You should register within 30 days after starting your activities or when you have reached the legal minimum income. This is currently € 1,080 per month[89]. If you are registered as a self-employed person in Spain, you pay a regular monthly fixed rate of € 294 per month. From 2023 onwards, a new system will apply: If you are registered as self-employed in Spain, you will pay a monthly quota calculated on the basis of your income, which will change every year until 2025 (in 2023, this will be between € 230 and € 500 per month). However, the first twelve months, this amount is reduced to 80 € per month.

In addition to the monthly fixed amount, income tax must also be paid. The amount of this tax is calculated based on your income. This classification is based on income modules. Taxes are paid per quarter and then later calculated based on an annual tax return. A tax advisor (*Gestor*) may be helpful to navigate the Spanish tax system and can also help you with your tax return. In my personal experience, preparing a tax return in Spain is generally somewhat manageable.

If you are registered as an Autónomo, you will have to charge your customers Spanish value added tax (*IVA*) on certain products and services. This is currently 21 %[90].

How to register as an autónomo

To be self-employed in Spain, you must register with the state within 30 days of starting your activities. The first step to self-employment is to register in the Spanish tax system to be able to pay the IAE (*Impuestos sobre las Actividades Económicos*) in the future. To do this, you must first make an appointment at the Hacienda. To register in the Spanish tax system, you will need the following documents:

- Completed document Modelo 036 or 037[91]
- NIE
- Passport or identity card and copy
- Spanish bank account

Now that you are registered, you should of course also inform the Social Security (*Seguridad Social*) about your new activities. There you have to take care of the RETA (*Régimen especial para trabajadores autónomos*). The following documents are required:

- Completed document Modelo 036 or 037
- NIE
- Passport or identity card and copy
- Registration Certificate (Certificado de Empadronamiento)
- IRPF (*Impuesto sobre la Renta de las Personas Físicas*) Tax Certificate

Getting in touch

One of the biggest challenges expats face when moving abroad is getting to know new people and making initial contacts locally. Those who come to the country for a semester abroad or a language course usually make connections quickly, even if only with other foreigners. However, entry aids can also be shared apartments or leisure activities. For example, finding a hobby or enrolling in a language course. Especially in big cities, there are activities almost every day where you can get in touch with new people. Many of these events are even free. A language exchange could be a great way to meet locals and get used to your new language. You can find such exchanges or other activities on platforms like Facebook, Meetup, and Couchsurfing.

Through Facebook and Couchsurfing, you can specifically look for people with similar interests to exchange ideas about your new home or go for a coffee together. If the language barrier is still too big at first, you can also specifically look for other (English-speaking) expats to make first acquaintances on the spot. There are simply countless opportunities to meet new people and make friends.

One experience I've had over the years, and that other expats tell me about time and time again, is that it can be difficult to build long-term, deep friendships in a new country. After all, it can sometimes be difficult for locals who already have their long-standing friendships in place to find time for you. In addition, there is a certain language barrier. Because even though it may only be a few months before you can speak the language, it will probably take a much longer time before you can really express your feelings and opinions as you would in your native language. International friends, on the other hand, don't always stay in the country long-term. Again and again, expats are drawn back to their home country. And so, it can sometimes take a while until really good friendships are formed in Spain. Despite everything, you should not give up hope, because those who seek will eventually find.

The Spanish education system

Schools in Spain

In general, there is compulsory schooling in Spain for ten years (from age 6 - 16). In the UK, on the other hand, kids must attend school from the summer after their 5th birthday until the end of June in the year of their 16th birthday. Meanwhile, in the US, the age of required school attendance years differs between the different states but is generally somewhere between five and 19 years of age.

Public or private school – which is the right one for your kids?

As with the UK and the US, there is a choice between learning in a public or a private school. In Spain, around 30 % of children attend a private school. Only about 7 % of British school-age children and approximately 10 % of all US children attend private schools. Many of the private schools in the country are run by the Catholic Church. However, children also can attend bilingual, trilingual, or even one of the international schools in Spain. International schools are especially popular with expat families because they follow international school systems. There are therefore also British and American schools that follow foreign curriculums in many places in the country. You can find a list of British, American, and other international schools in Spain in the related links[92]. Among expatriate families who are only temporarily staying in the country, international schools are therefore especially popular, as they follow the foreign school guidelines. In general, the prices of

Spain's schools differ significantly. While public schools are free of charge for children from 3 to 18 years of age and only the costs of the required school materials must be paid, the tuition at private schools usually has a high price. € 500 per month per child for attending an international school is thus no rarity.

Each of these types of schools offers its advantages and disadvantages. While private schools often teach in smaller classes, offer a broader range of extracurricular activities, and come with a higher budget for teaching materials, public schools can be a practical way for your children to integrate into Spain and learn the language. Of course, the cost of the different school systems is also an important factor. For older children, it may also be wise to involve the children themselves in the decision-making process. In general, the following questions may be helpful in finding the right school:

- In which language will the lessons take place?
- Which languages will/can my child learn during their school years?
- What knowledge/subjects are included in the curriculum?
- What degree will my child receive at the end of their school career? Is the degree internationally recognized?
- How is the school schedule?
- What are the extracurricular activities offered?
- What costs will I incur?

The thing with the language

As just mentioned, the language spoken in class may differ depending on the school or the type of school chosen. This is true not only for private schools but also for local schools. The reason for this is that in some regions of Spain, another official language is spoken in addition to Castilian. In these regions, it is possible that the second official language of the region is primarily used as the language of instruction in the schools. You should therefore inquire about the language used in class before enrolling your child in a school. However, for children, the second language in class does not have to be a disadvantage. On the contrary, in fact, by using the second official language at school, children have a great opportunity to learn the language and later be able to speak and use it fluently without any problems.

A friend of mine who grew up in Barcelona, even though both of her parents were originally from other Spanish-speaking areas, told me how happy she is to have learned Catalan in school because today she speaks the language at a native level, and that's despite the fact that neither of her parents speak Catalan.

The Spanish school system

The Spanish school system is not all that dissimilar to the US and the UK.

While the Spanish central government sets the general educational guidelines, the individual autonomous regions of Spain can determine the details. There can therefore be differences in the education system between the country's individual areas.

On a typical school day, afternoon classes are not uncommon, even for young students. In this respect, children usually eat lunch in the school cafeteria instead of going home for lunch. This can be a welcome change, especially for working parents. A typical Spanish school day runs from around 9:00 am to 4:30 pm.

In general, the compulsory Spanish school system consists of three blocks:

Educación Primaria is equivalent to British primary school and elementary school in the US. Children start in first grade at age six and stay until sixth grade.

After that, they continue with **Eduación Secundaria Obligatoria**, or *ESO* for short. This type of school corresponds to secondary school in the UK and junior high school in the US. The ESO is obligatory for all Spanish children and takes four years to complete.

The ESO certificate can be compared to finishing senior school in the UK. Now the children choose whether they want to attend the upper school (*Bachillerato*) with the subsequent Bachillerato graduation or start vocational training (*Formación Profesional*). In the upper school, students can then specialize in an area (e.g., natural sciences or languages). After two years, upper school is completed with the Bachillerato. This corresponds to college in the UK or (senior) high school in the US and allows access to university.

If you choose professional vocational training in Spain, it does not occur in a company but at school. However, practical knowledge is also imparted to the trainees during various internships. Unfortunately, these internships are generally not remunerated. A distinction is made between ***Formación Profesional de Grado Medio*** and ***Formación Profesional de Grado Superior***. The Formación de Grado Medio lasts two years and ends with the title *Técnico*. However, higher degree-professional training can only be chosen after completing the Bachillerato or subsequently to the first training. At the end of the Grado Superior training, the trainee is then allowed to use the title *Técnico Superior*. With the Técnico Superior, the trainee also has the opportunity to attend university.

The grading system in Spain also differs from that in the US and the UK. While US children are graded with letters and children in England are used to grades from one to nine, Spanish children are graded with a point system from zero to ten, with ten being the best score. Moreover, grades in Spain are not given every six months, but every three months.

Enrollment in a Spanish School

Regular registration of children at a new school takes place in March. However, if you move during the current school year, you can typically register your children at that time as well. After all, school attendance is compulsory, provided there are still enough places available at the school of your choice. You can find out exactly which documents are required to enroll in the school of your choice by contacting the school directly or the town hall (*Ayuntamiento*) of the city. In general, the following documents are required:

- Proof of residence (e.g., rental contract or padrón)
- Passport of the parents
- Passport of the child
- Birth certificate of the child
- Proof of the child's required vaccinations (vaccination card) - some schools also require a health certificate of the child

Eduación Infantil – Education of the youngest family members

Spain also offers sufficient education and childcare for the youngest children (*Preescolar*). The program is divided into two cycles. Between the ages of three months and three years, parents can have their children looked after in what is called a *Guardería*. Since only up to 16 weeks of parental leave are provided in Spain, care in the Guardería is often taken up by working parents.

Afterward, children between the ages of three and six can attend preschool (*Escuela Infantil*). Although attendance here is voluntary, about 98 % of Spanish children between the ages of three and five attend preschool. For children of expats, this can be the perfect time to become familiar with the language and culture of the country before starting school. Like the kindergarten in your country, there is plenty of time to play and make friends. Nevertheless, Spanish preschool is also about learning. Here, the children are introduced to numbers and letters in a playful way. Some can already read and solve the first simple arithmetic problems when they start school.

University and higher studies in Spain

Anyone who finished their high school or high school-like degree in the US, UK, or the EU can theoretically study at a university in Spain. While the UK is still treated as an EU member when it comes to recognizing their college degrees (however, this might change shortly), you might need to have your American high school diploma recognized in Spain before enrolling in a Spanish university course. The main factor is the classes you took in high school and which university in the country you want to enroll in. Make sure to check with the individual university before starting the application process to be on the safe side. Since the 2010 Bologna Process, what is called the *Eduación Superior* in Spain has been divided into bachelor's and master's degree programs to be comparable with other European countries. Nevertheless, the old titles are still frequently used in linguistic usage. Accordingly, the Bachelor corresponds to the *Diplomatura*, the Master to the *Licenciatura*, or the Doctor to the *Doctorado*.

Although the bachelor's and master's degrees are equated with European degrees, the length of study may differ between different European countries. Accordingly, the Bachelor's degree in Spain usually lasts about four years, while the Master's degree is usually awarded after only one or two years of study.

Full study or semester abroad

Basically, there are different ways to study in Spain. On the one hand, you can complete full-time study in the country or apply exclusively for a semester abroad or a summer school.

The time and cost factor of the different options is an especially important decision criterion. In most cases, a semester abroad is chosen because it only lasts a few months, and you will receive application assistance from your regular university. However, if you really want to immerse yourself in the culture of the country and get to know real Spanish life, you should probably also think about the possibility of a complete study in Spain.

In general, both complete courses of study and individual courses completed in Spain can subsequently be credited and recognized in all of the EU.

Types and fields of study at the universities

Most of the time, students in Spain study at a traditional university. The majority of universities in the country are state institutions. However, there is also the option of studying at one of the private universities. These are often better equipped but also a lot more expensive. There are also some Escuelas Universitarias, which are pretty similar to the standard universities but independent from them.

There is a large selection of specializations and

courses of study. It is generally unusual to move for studies in Spain if you already live in a university town. This means that it is quite possible to find all fields of study in the country's major cities. As a result, the average Spaniard is already 29.5 years old when they first leave Hotel Mama and stand on their own two feet. (By comparison, the EU average is 25.9 years, while the average Brit leave home at 24.6 years and the average American at 23.4 years of age)[93].

Admission to university

The academic year takes place from September to June and is divided into two semesters. The application process, as well as the application period, can differ depending on the university. You should therefore inquire about the application process at the university of your choice in good time and prepare the relevant documents.

If you wish to pursue a bachelor's degree in Spain, you might first have your high school diploma, baccalaureate, or other university entrance qualification accredited by the Spanish distance learning university, *Universidad Nacional de Educación a Distancia* (UNED), through its UNEDassis body (if you do not have a Spanish high school diploma). You can find more information about this process in the related links[94].

Some colleges and universities also reserve the right to require an aptitude test for their applicants. Others expect proof of the applicant's language skills, such as a DELE certificate if the course is Spanish or the second regional official language. Other application criteria may include letters of motivation or recommendation. Also, some universities charge an application fee.

If you want to come to Spain exclusively for a semester abroad or a summer school, you should already be enrolled at a university at the beginning of the application process. Your own university can also help you with the application process.

Study costs

The cost of studying generally depends on the university and the chosen field of study. Study costs at the state universities vary significantly, depending on the region, with Andalusia being the cheapest region and Catalonia the most expensive. The national average price for a bachelor's degree is around € 1,000 per year. While in Andalusia, you pay less than € 800, in Catalonia, you may have to pay up to € 2,400 per year. For a Master's degree, you should calculate up to € 4,000 per year. Studying at a private university will most likely be much more expensive - € 10,000 per year for studying at a private university is not uncommon. The tuition fees can be found on the respective university's website and are usually given in euros per credit (*créditos*). In addition to the tuition fees, you will also have to pay examination and registration fees.

Along with the tuition fees, you will also have to pay for your accommodation, transportation, activities, and daily needs. You should not budget too tightly. If you are only in the country to study, you will certainly want to do a lot. The cost of living depends on the region of Spain you choose. In the cities of Barcelona and Madrid especially, you should expect high rental prices. If you like it a bit cheaper, you can choose what is called a Residencia, a student accommodation. Here you not only have the opportunity to get in contact with other students, but you can also select the option of half board.

If you enroll only for one semester abroad, you should expect higher costs for one semester. The price also includes the student social program and on-site support. Accordingly, you should expect to pay around € 1,000 to € 4,000 per semester. In addition, you should, of course, also plan for ongoing costs for rent and general living expenses.

Financial aid for your studies

Those who cannot finance their dream of studying abroad on their own may have the opportunity to receive financial aid. One possibility is to apply for a scholarship. For example, if you graduated from high school with honors, you might have a good chance of enrolling in a Spanish university free of charge. In general, there are various scholarships worldwide that emphasize different aspects. It is best to find out on the internet which options are available for you.

Another possibility for financing your studies or semester abroad could be different kinds of grants. There are different options depending on what country you are from, and what and where you plan to study. Make sure you check in the related links[95] and check for further options with your university or online.

Further assistance for financing your studies can be educational loans.

First 3 months after your arrival in Spain

Residencia (Only for EU-passport holders)

After three months in Spain at the latest, it is mandatory for EU passport holders to register as a resident in the country. You can do this by registering in the Central Registry of Foreigners (Registro Central de Extranjeros). As a result, you will automatically receive the Residencia Card (Certificado de Registro de Ciudadano de la Unión). This card is used in the country to identify yourself as a resident of Spain. The Residencia card is only valid in conjunction with your identity card or passport. Since it does not contain a photo of you, it cannot be used as a photo ID.

Europeans only receive the Residencia card, but not the TIE card. The latter is reserved for non-European citizens as a sort of residence permit.

However, the green Residencia card is only a small piece of green paper. The card must therefore be well protected, as the writing comes off very easily and the card generally wears out quickly. Unfortunately, shrink-wrapping the paper is not allowed.

The difference between NIE and Residencia

Although the application for residencia is often associated with the NIE application process, these are fundamentally two distinct processes. Often the actual NIE is referred to as a temporary NIE, while the Residencia is often referred to as a permanent (green)

NIE.

This is because when you apply for the NIE, you only receive your tax number, not your resident certificate. So, you can apply for an NIE without having an official residence in Spain (e.g., if you want to buy a property in the country). The Residencia, on the other hand, certifies that you have residency in Spain. Many processes (e.g., taking out an insurance policy) require the Residencia card. When you are asked by the authorities for your NIE, in most cases they are talking about the Residencia card.

While theoretically anyone can apply for the NIE, the Residencia is subject to one or more of the following conditions:

- You must either be registered in Spain as an employee (employment contract and Informe de Vida Laboral must be submitted)
- Be registered as a self-employed person (Autónomo) in Spain
- Be registered in Spain as a student
- Have close family members registered as residents
- Or have sufficient financial means (around € 6,000 in a bank account to your name)

How to apply for Residencia

The process to apply for residencia is similar to the process to apply for an NIE.

- Get an appointment (*Cita Previa*) online Monday morning at 8 am*
- Bring the following documents to the appointment
    - o The application document (No. 18)[96]

- o Passport and copy of passport or ID card and copy of ID card
- o NIE (original document)
- o Social Security document (original)
- o Empadronamiento document (not older than three months)
- o Employment contract, enrollment certificate, or bank statement with enough money in it (at least € 6,000 per person)
- o Document about the payment of the fee (No. 790[97])
- o Informe de La Vida Laboral (they might or might not ask for it, so it's better to have it with you. You can receive it from the Social Security).
- If you do not speak Spanish, it is best to take someone with you to translate - almost no one speaks English.
- Check your data after receiving the documents

* Lately, it seems to be quite a struggle to get an appointment. I recommend using the app and trying from 8 am for several hours until it shows available dates. The application process is the same as when you applied for your NIE.

1. Open the website[98] in your browser or in the app *Cita Previa Extranjería*[99] (recommended)
2. Select your province and click on *Aceptar*
3. Select *Policia - Certificados UE*, and then click *Aceptar*
4. Click on *Entrar*
5. Enter your NIE, passport, or ID card number
6. Enter your name and surname

7. Select the country of your citizenship (e.g., *Alemania* for Germany)
8. Then click on *Aceptar*
9. Now click on *Solicitar Cita*
10. Now you can either choose a date or you will be informed that there are no appointments available at the moment - if that's the case, try again later.

Registering your car

If you plan to stay in the country for more than six months, you will also need to register your car in Spain. Generally, registering your vehicle is anything but cheap and takes a lot of time. It is therefore best to determine whether you really need your car locally before you move. In big cities, especially during rush hour, it is often faster to get from A to B by relying on public transportation such as the metro. Depending on the age and condition of your car, it may even be cheaper to sell your car and buy a new one in Spain instead.

Also, be careful with the registration process because it can get costly depending on the registration date and vehicle model. Depending on your car's CO_2 emissions per km, an import tax is due upon registration in the country. This tax can be up to 14.75 % of the table value of your car. But don't worry, there are two ways you can avoid this high tax and save a lot of money:

If your vehicle is a small car that produces less than 120 g/km of CO_2, it is exempt from the import tax. Another option to avoid paying the import tax is if your car has been in your possession for at least six months before registration in Spain and has been registered in another EU country for at least twelve months in total. However, your car must be registered within two months after your registration in Spain. In addition, a certificate from your embassy or consulate your car has previously been registered in is necessary. The name of the certificate might differ depending on the country so it's best to call and ask the staff for information. Expect to pay about € 25. In any case, you are on the safe side if you get advice from a Gestoría. They can also take care of the registration process for you for an additional fee of € 200 to 400.

If you decide to register your car in Spain yourself, the following steps are necessary:

Registering your car in Spain – step-by-step

The first step to registering your car in Spain is the **homologación**. This is done by a technical engineer (*Perito*). Check with a garage or car dealer for contacts. You need the *Certificado de Características*. This document costs around € 120.

The next step to register your car in Spain is the registration by the Spanish Technical Control Board. This is called ITV (*Inspección Técnica de Vehículos*) in Spain. There you should ask for the *Ficha Técnica Española*[100]. It is advisable to request an appointment (*Cita Previa*) to avoid long waiting times. Below you will find all the information and links to request an appointment[101]. On the day of your appointment, you should have the following documents ready:

- Vehicle registration document
- Certificado de Características
- NIE
- Certificado de Empadronamiento
- EC Certificate of Conformity (also known as COC (*Certificate of Conformity*) or CE (*Certificado de conformidad*) - this document can be issued to you by your car manufacturer for a fee of around € 100

After the ITV has registered your car, the registration tax (*Impuesto de Matriculación*) is due at the local tax office (*Hacienda*). In addition, the vehicle tax (*Impuesto sobre vehículos de tracción mecánica*) is due at the town hall (*Ayuntamiento*) in your city.

After taking all the steps described above, you can finally apply for your Permiso de Circulación, i.e., your driver's permission, at the vehicle registration office (*Tráfico*). You will find the documents you need for the registration there. The administrative fee will cost you another € 91.

In order to be allowed to drive on the roads of Spain, you should now take out car insurance with a provider of your choice. After that, all you need is a license plate for your car.

Congratulations, your car is now registered in Spain, and you have done all the paperwork. If you have not yet deregistered your vehicle in your country, you can do so through the embassy or the nearest consulate.

Exchange or get a driver's license

Anyone who has lived in Spain for more than two years is obliged to have their driver's license converted into a Spanish driver's license or get a new Spanish driver's license (for most-non-EU countries, the limit is six months). Those who forget to have their driver's license changed will have to pay a fee of € 200. Exempt from this rule are all those who received a European driver's license after 19.01.2013. If this is the case, your driver's license is also valid in Spain until the expiration date, thanks to the new European regulation. This regulation also applies if you already exchanged your regular European driver's license for a new driver's license after 2013. Bad news for everyone holding a non-EU driver's license – you most probably will have to take a theoretical and practical driving test before getting a

Spanish driver's license. However, there are some exceptions. You can find the countries that can keep their own driver's license in the further links[102] (the UK and the US are not among them).

The Spanish driver's license must generally be renewed every ten years until the age of 65. After the age of 65, the driver's license is then only valid for five years at a time. In order to renew your driver's license in Spain, you must also pass a vision and fitness test. The fitness test can be done under the name "*informe de aptitud psicofísico*" in a medical facility.

If you are allowed to exchange your driver's license, you can do so at the Road Traffic Office (*General de Tráfico*). First, an appointment (*cita previa*) is necessary. You can find the website where you can get an appointment in the links below[103]. On the day of your appointment, you should show up with the following documents:

- Driver's license and copy (front and back)
- Residencia (green NIE card) and copy
- Copy of passport
- Empadronamiento (not older than three months)
- 2 passport photos (Spanish size: 32 x 26 mm)
- Medical certificate
- Fee of about € 50 in cash

The exchange process can take several weeks to months, depending on the municipality. Currently, you should expect up to ten months, depending on the region. In the meantime, you will receive a temporary driver's license. However, this one is only valid within Spain.

If you want to avoid long waiting times, you also have the option of commissioning a Gestoría with the exchange process.

If you have to take the driver's test, you can apply for it on the official DGT website[104].

Recommendations and tips for expats

Before you start preparing for your big adventure in Spain, I would like to give you some helpful tips along the way. For this purpose, I have asked an important question in expat groups online and during various interviews with other Spain expats (you can find the link to the interviews in the links below[105]): *"What would you have liked to know before moving to Spain?"*

Learn Spanish before moving

If there were only one thing I could recommend to you, it would be to learn a bit of Spanish before you set off on your Spanish adventure. It helps immensely to get connected in the country and go through all the annoying bureaucratic processes if you have at least some basic knowledge of Spanish. If you already have some language learning experience, free tools like Duolingo or grammar websites can be helpful. Otherwise, you can enroll in a course at night school, language school, or online.

If you've studied Spanish before, it can be helpful to brush up on your language skills before you leave using podcasts, language learning videos, or a language exchange.

August is probably the worst month to move to Spain

Have you ever tried to get anything done in Spain in August? If so, you probably know why August is not the best month to get settled in your new adopted country.

In August, Spain is like a deserted place.

While the tourist crowds in the country peak every year in August, Spaniards also like to take some time off. You will therefore quickly notice that many stores, businesses, and government offices remain closed during this month. Going to the authorities or anything else that needs to be done is therefore almost impossible in August.

Find the right timing to move to save taxes

I have already recommended several times in this book to check with a professional tax consultant or at least with someone who knows a lot about taxes before you move abroad. For US citizens, it can have even more benefits to plan your move according to the tax law in order to save quite a considerable amount in taxes. Because if you stay abroad for at least 330 days within a consecutive 12-month period in a tax year (January to December), i.e., passing the Bona Fide Resident Test[106], you might be able to make use of the Foreign Earned Income Tax Exclusion[107]. This process could help you exclude around up to $ 100,000 from US taxation.

Don't wait for the perfect moment to come

"If we wait until we're ready, we'll be waiting for the rest of our lives" – Lemony Snicket

Some emigrants wait far too long before finally taking the plunge to start a new life in Spain. In fact, 59-year-old emigrant Marion revealed to me in our emigrant interview that she waited almost 40 years to finally move to her dream destination in Gran Canaria. She even described returning to Germany after her first stay as the *"biggest mistake in [her] life."*

Undoubtedly, such an important decision should not simply be rushed, and of course, extensive preparation for moving abroad is part of it. Nevertheless, you should not put off this intention for too long if you suspect that Spain is the right choice for you. Sometimes you just have to jump into the deep end. I hope, however, that this book will help you to land softly.

Inform yourself

Information is the be-all and end-all of moving abroad and is therefore simply indispensable. Since you already have this book in your hands, you are definitely on the right track. Information about the TIE process and similar bureaucratic matters can save you a lot of time and nerves. Information about the country and culture, on the other hand, can be useful to help you make connections more quickly and avoid putting your foot in your mouth.

You can find information online in emigration forums, blogs, and Google. For most regions of Spain, you will be able to find Facebook groups using the search function. Here you can ask all the questions you might have and exchange ideas with other travelers and expatriates.

Corruption and scams

When I asked in a Barcelona expats group what the one thing was that immigrants would have liked to know beforehand, I was quite surprised how clearly two answers emerged. The first popular answer is the chaotic bureaucracy in the country, which has already been mentioned a time or two in this book. The second frequently expressed answer is corruption and rip-offs.

First of all, you should note that Spain is not really more dangerous than other EU states. Nevertheless, some laws in the country make corruption and rip-offs easy in many respects. Here, especially pickpockets and what are called Okupas are to be mentioned. Spain and especially the Catalan capital Barcelona are increasingly becoming a paradise for pickpockets. If they are caught with less than € 400, they do not have to expect any further legal consequences.

Also, you should have heard about the Spanish legislation concerning the Okupas at least once before you sign a lease or acquire real estate. If illegal squatters, called Okupas, gain access to your house or apartment, you have only 48 hours to get rid of them. If you do not manage to evict the squatters from your home within this time, it can be a real tragedy to reclaim your home. Vigilante actions, such as using violence or changing the locks, can even result in heavy fines or jail time for you. Even the police will most likely be of little help. This is because there is a "*right to dignified housing*" in Spain. It's just quite bad luck if the Okupas have chosen your property as their dignified living space. Most of the time, the only solution is legal action for eviction, which can take several months or even years.

Facebook groups

Another great tip that I can't stress enough is Facebook groups. No matter what question you have about life in Spain, there is sure to be someone who has had a similar problem in the past and will be happy to help you. Facebook groups are also beneficial for getting to know other expats and can make it easier for you to get started in your new home country.

To find a suitable group, simply use the Facebook search function and enter terms such as "*[Your country's people] in [place or region in Spain]*", e.g., "*Americans/Expats in Barcelona*". If your location is too small or unknown among emigrants, you will certainly be in good hands in the groups "Spain's Help Group for Expats" or similar.

What else you should know about life in Spain – cultural particularities

For some, the cultural differences between their country and Spain are even one of the main reasons to emigrate to the Iberian Peninsula. For others, some of the country's cultural peculiarities are more of a hurdle to overcome. Whether you see the traditions and customs as an obstacle or an advantage, it is important that you know and respect the Spanish way of life if you decide to live under the Spanish sun. Ideally, you will not only get used to Spanish ways, but you will even become a part of them. Because only in this way can you really go from being a guest in the country to a real local of Spain.

Greetings with kisses

Typical of southern Europe, people in Spain also usually greet each other with two hinted kisses on the cheek. Even when meeting new people, this is the accepted procedure for introducing oneself. While a regular handshake, on the other hand, seems rather cold or dismissive, it is nevertheless often used in business circles. If you are unsure how to greet your counterpart, it is best to wait until they make the first move.

If you make new acquaintances in your circle of friends, however, it is predominantly greeted with kisses. Here, a kiss on each cheek is indicated (starting on the left). This means that you do not actually kiss your counterpart on the cheek but rather breathe the kiss into the air on the cheek of your partner. Men, however, do not usually greet each other with a kiss but with a handshake or a hug, depending on the level of relationship.

Admittedly, at first, for me, it also took some time getting used to always greeting strangers with a kiss. On hot days in particular, you always meet that one sweaty person you'd probably rather greet with a good old handshake (or not touching them at all). However, you get used to this Spanish greeting after only a short time, which makes a handshake suddenly seem entirely unfamiliar to you the next time you visit home.

Daily routine and understanding of time

In Spain, the clocks tick differently. And I am not talking about the time difference between the countries. While most Westerners are already sitting diligently in the office, the Spaniard turns over once again with pleasure in his bed. Only a few jobs start earlier than 8:30 or 9:00 in the morning. Accordingly, the Spaniards spend longer in the office.

While John Doe has already eaten the sandwich he brought with him to work and is back at his desk, Juan Pérez finally takes his well-earned one to two-hour lunch break between 1 and 2 pm. Although more and more Spaniards are switching to bringing their own food from home, many still use their entire lunch break by ordering a menú del día with their colleagues at a nearby restaurant. As a result, these lunch menus are often well-priced and consist of an appetizer, one or two main courses, drink, and dessert.

While the average John Doe is already sitting down to dinner, Spaniards can then finally call it a day between 6 and 8 pm. On the other hand, dinner is only served between 9 and 10 pm in Spain. Many restaurants, therefore, don't even open in the evening until 8 pm - except, of course, in the tourist areas, where we foreigners can also eat at foreign dinner times.

The siesta

In Spanish, the siesta is usually equated with the midday nap and therefore refers to the time when stores in Spain traditionally close during the afternoon, usually between 2 and 5 pm. While the siesta was ubiquitous up until a few years ago, it is now gradually retreating from the Spanish workplace. The lunch break in an average company is usually around one to two hours, making it not worthwhile for workers to go home for a midday nap.

The siesta was once introduced due to the hot temperatures during the afternoon hours. For this reason, it is still more widespread in the south of the country than in the north. In general, however, a decline in the siesta can be seen throughout Spain. In fact, usually, only smaller stores close their doors during the midday hours. Some companies also adopt the siesta tradition only in August.

The royal family

While you probably can't flip through a newspaper at a hairdresser's without coming across a photo of the English royal family, many people aren't really aware that Spain also has a king. The Spanish king, Rey Felipe VI, is the country's official head of state but performs mostly representative duties.

However, since the royal family is not equally popular with all Spaniards, you might want to avoid the topic with locals if you don't want to start a political discussion.

Family names

You've probably heard the cliché that people from Spanish-speaking countries always have such long names. There is definitely some truth to this prejudice. By law alone, every Spaniard already has two surnames. If a second name is added to their first name, the name is much longer than we are used to in most other Western countries.

The surname of a Spaniard is usually composed of the first surname of their father and the first surname of their mother. For this reason, the full names of both parents must still be indicated on many Spanish documents, even in adulthood.

However, upon marriage, Spaniards then retain their surnames. When looking at the surnames, it is therefore not possible to tell whether a couple is married or not. Nevertheless, Juan Pérez and his wife María Sánchez, on the other hand, are often referred to by acquaintances as Los Pérez or Familia Pérez, even though Maria has officially kept her maiden name. This example also shows that the second surname is often not used colloquially. On official documents, however, both surnames must always be indicated.

Similar to some German and Scandinavian surnames, many common Spanish surnames (almost all surnames ending in -z) can be traced back to their ancestors' first names. For example, the name Pérez originated from "son of Pedro" or Rodríguez from "son of Rodrigo". There is also some truth in the cliché that almost everyone in Spain has the same last name. The most common surnames in the country are García, González, Rodríguez, Fernández, López, Martínez, Sánchez, Pérez, Gómez, Martín, Jiménez, Ruiz, Hernández and Díaz. More than a third of Spain has at least one of these surnames. I, too, have one of these names since my marriage to my husband, Eduardo. If you marry a Spaniard as a foreign citizen and it's common in your country to change your last name upon marriage, you usually have the choice of keeping your surname according to Spanish law or taking the surname of your partner according to your country's law. However, this can lead to problems with Spanish registry offices. If you wish to take your partner's surnames, it is therefore advisable to marry in your country. By the way, some foreign states do not allow Spanish surnames to be separated. This means you can only take the full surnames or keep your own surname. So, you as John Doe can continue to call yourself John Doe or John Sánchez Gómez after your marriage with María Sánchez Gómez. John Sánchez or even a combination of both surnames like John Doe Sánchez or John Sánchez Doe is often not allowed.

Tipping in Spain

While in the US, we tip as a matter of course when we pay for our meal in a restaurant or beer in a pub, tipping, or *propina* as the Spanish call it, is reserved for exceptional service similar to the UK. You can therefore decide for yourself if you want to tip or not, without it being assumed by the person attending you.

The tip is also not given directly when paying as in the US. First, you get the full amount of the change back. Then, you can leave a few coins or bills behind when you leave or give them directly to the waiter.

Splitting the bill

Another peculiarity is that restaurant bills in Spain are usually paid per table and not per person. Although it is common for smaller groups to pay separately, larger groups almost always pay together. In most cases, the bill is either divided by the number of group members, or the entire bill is paid in turn by different group members.

Bread with your meal

The Spanish love white bread. Bread is therefore

served with almost every meal. Even with rice or pasta, many Spaniards eat bread. Some even keep a piece of bread in their hand throughout the meal, which they dip into the sauce. However, if you dip a piece of bread into the soup, as is common in many Western countries, you definitely earn confused looks from the Spaniards.

When we speak of bread in Spain, it is usually baguette or similar white bread.

Spain does not equal Spain

When you think of Spain, you probably first have the typical image of bullfights and flamenco in mind. The truth is, however, that depending on which region of Spain you visit, the culture that awaits you there can be quite different. Just as many foreign tourists expect Texan barbecues and cowboy boots and then are quite confused when they visit New York or California or tea time and rainy weather in the UK... oh wait, you do have that all over the UK...never mind. The cultural differences between the various Spanish regions even go so far that you can get the feeling you have landed in a completely different culture when you travel back and forth between the individual provinces. For example, these differences become evident when you travel from Basque Country to Andalusia.

However, not only the lifestyle and architecture but also the weather, the food, and the prices differ greatly in the individual regions. While the Spanish north is relatively expensive by national standards, in Andalusia, you often pay only a small fraction of what you would pay in the Basque Country, for example.

We have already talked about linguistic differences at the beginning of this book. Besides the second official languages of some regions, however, the Spanish dialect also changes depending on which part of the country you are in. Arguably the most neutral Spanish is spoken in Madrid and Castile and Leon, while Andalusia and especially Cadiz are notorious for their strong dialect.

Colloquial language is not for the faint of heart

The Spanish love their expletives. And so there are dozens of types of expletives and swear words in Spain that slip casually into regular conversation. I only really became aware of the obscene use of language in Spain during our five-month trip to South America. My husband Eduardo regularly earned confused or even shocked looks when his typical Spanish vocabulary came out too much when talking to locals. Given the wide range of common vulgar expressions, every Spaniard even seems to have their personal favorites they use repeatedly.

Whether you adopt the expressions into your own vernacular is up to you. You would sound typically Spanish. However, you should not take the sometimes offensive terms literally or personally. Even if these expressions may seem strange at first, in most cases, none of the words is really meant as an insult. A large part of these vulgar words has now become part of everyday speech in such a way that the literal meaning is usually no longer perceived as such when spoken. Because once you translate some of these statements literally, it can be really shocking how often they are used in everyday life. My personal favorite, by the way, is the expression "*Me cago en la leche*", which translates as "I s*it in the milk".

Aside from the colloquialisms used, the volume factor adds to any conversation in Spain. Spaniards are known for their passionate conversations, so it can get quite loud. If you visit restaurants or bars in the country, you should definitely get used to the new volume level. Even today, it sometimes happens to me that I simply can't be heard in conversations with my German reserve.

Sobremesa

It is well known that Spaniards spend a lot of time together with family and friends because in Spanish culture, nothing beats the Familia. On weekends and holidays, people often sit together for hours, eating and drinking together. Spaniards love sitting together after meals so much that there is even a word for it in the Spanish vocabulary: *Sobremesa*. Translated into English, this concept means something like "*over the table*." After a long and heavy meal in particular, this time is used for a coffee or shot while having long conversations or watching TV together. Especially popular topics of conversation are politics and religion, which already brings us to the next topic.

Politics and religion

While we Germans often avoid topics such as politics and religion, especially if we cannot yet assess the views of our counterpart, it can happen already when getting to know Spaniards that these topics come up and are discussed passionately. Again and again, however, this also leads to arguments since the political and religious views in the country are sometimes far apart. Particularly in the autonomous regions of Catalonia, Galicia, and the Basque Country, political opinions are widely divided. So if you want to avoid a political discussion, it's probably best not to bring up this topic. The same applies to bullfighting, by the way.

Spanish houses

If you are invited to a Spaniard's home, you should definitely ask about the apartment because on the doorbell signs usually only the apartment numbers are indicated, but not the names of the residents. Also, the division of the floors differs from other countries' way of counting. When you enter the house, you are in the

Planta Baja, which is also abbreviated as PB. In many houses, the Planta Principal (PP) follows instead of the second floor. Counting from one upwards only takes place from the next floor. The top floor is called *Ático*.

FAQ about living in Spain

How LGBTQI+-friendly is Spain?

Spain is considered one of the most open countries to the LGBTQI+ community, with many laws that benefit homosexuals and transgender people. According to a survey, more than 88 % of Spaniards accept homosexuals, making the country one of the most LGBTQI+ friendly countries in the world. Spain was one of the first countries in the EU to allow same-sex marriages back in 2005. By comparison, same-sex marriages have only been officially permitted in the US since 2015 and in the UK since 2014. Additionally, many bars, beaches, and even entire cities, such as the small town of Sitges on the Costa Dorada, have specifically adapted to the LGBTQI+ scene.

Is life in Spain expensive?

In itself, life in Spain is cheaper than in the UK and the US. On average, the difference can be up to 45 %. However, it should be said that salaries in Spain are also lower on average than in the US and the UK. If you live in expensive cities like Madrid and Barcelona, you also have to expect high rents. Accordingly, you can't say 100 % across the board whether and how much cheaper life is in Spain because it all depends on where and how you live.

How many expats live in Spain?

While there are no official numbers, it is assumed that there are around 5.5 million expats living in Spain. Approximately 280,000 of those are British and about

40,000 are from the US.

Can I live in Spain without the NIE?

Anyone staying in the country for more than three months is required by law to register in the population register. This process is carried out in Spain with the application for residencia or the TIE. In order to apply for the Residencia, the NIE is required. Accordingly, it is not possible to live in Spain without an NIE. However, those who stay fewer than three months, do not work in the country, or want to sign contracts can do so without the NIE.

Is it always warm in Spain?

Like many, you might have this typical image of Spain as a permanently warm country where the sun always shines. Although the sun shines much more often on average in Spain than it does in most other European countries, and it rains only a few hours a year, depending on the location, there are four seasons in Spain, just like in the UK and most parts of the US. Exceptions to this are the Canary Islands, which have a subtropical climate all year round, with temperatures varying by only a few degrees over the course of the year. However, in the rest of the country, it inevitably gets cold in winter. Temperatures vary according to region and location. For example, while winters on the coast tend to be mild, other parts of the country may even experience snowfall. So, when moving to Spain, you might not want to forget packing your winter jacket.

Can I move to Spain without money?

While researching this book, I kept coming across the question of whether it was possible to move without money. I think that we should distinguish here whether it is feasible or smart to emigrate to Spain without any cash. Besides the fact that most visa options require proof of sufficient funds, I can only strongly recommend everyone to move to Spain only with a saved money buffer that can keep you afloat in the country for at least six months, ideally longer. You should also have enough savings set aside at all times to be able to return home in case of an emergency. Even if you have an employment contract in your pocket before you leave, you should never be too sure. In Spain, you are only entitled to state subsidies or aid after you have worked in the country for at least twelve months.

Apart from that, I have met emigrants who went to Spain without any savings. I particularly remember a colleague from my first job, let's call him Jack. Jack came to Barcelona from England with no savings and initially stayed free of charge with a cousin who lived in the city. In the very first month, he had to ask our boss for an advance to make ends meet. When his cousin then gave him an ultimatum to find his own place to stay, Jack had to borrow even more money to pay the security payments to the landlord. Of course, the day our work project was closed down from one day to another, and we lost our jobs, panic set in. Although I haven't had any contact with Jack since then, I know through social media that he still lives in Barcelona. So it may well be possible to emigrate to Spain without money, but whether this state of affairs is desirable remains questionable.

How about living in Spain as a vegetarian?

I have to admit, living in Spain as a vegetarian can be quite a challenge, but it is doable. The Spaniards love meat, fish, and seafood, and so even salads are sometimes served with tuna or meat side dishes. Despite all this, there are now more and more people who follow the vegetarian lifestyle. In big cities especially, you can find more and more vegetarian restaurants and options in the supermarket. However, those who eat out in small towns, villages, or traditional restaurants often only have a choice between fish and meat. If this is the case, it can be helpful to specifically ask the waiter for vegetarian options.

Helpful Words for successful Registration in Spain

¿Cómo te llamas? – What's your name?

¿Cuánto cuesta...? – How much does...cost?

¿Dónde está el baño? – Where is the bathroom?

¿Dónde está...? – Where is...?

¿Habla/s inglés? – Do you speak English?

¿Lo entiendes? – Do you understand?

¿Puede/s hablar más despacio, por favor? – Could you speak slower, please?

¿Puede/s repetirlo? – Could you repeat that?

¿Qué significa...? – What does...mean?

Adiós – Goodbye

Apellidos* - Last Names (*Usually used in Plural since Spaniards have two last names)

Ayuntamiento - Townhall

Buenos días – Good Day

Cajero automático – ATM

Casado/a – married

Ciudad – City

Código Postal – Zip Code

Correo electrónico - E-mail address

Dirección – Address

Edad – Age

El banco – The banc

Estado – State

Estados Unidos – United States

Fecha de nacimiento – Date of Birth

Gracias – Thank you

Hola – Hello

Hospital – Hospital

Inglaterra - England

Lugar de nacimiento – Place of birth

Me gusta... - I like...

Me llamo... - My name is...

Nacionalidad – Nationality

Necesito ayuda – I need help

No entiendo – I don't understand

No sé – I don't know

Nombre – Name

Número de teléfono – Telephone number

País - Country

Perdón – Excuse me

Policía – Police

Por Favor – Please

Quiero... - I want...

Reino Unido – United Kingdom

Sexo – Gender

Vegetariano – Vegetarian

Important Telephone Numbers and Foreign Representation

Emergency numbers within Spain

Police: 112, 091 (national Police) or 092 local Police

Ambulance: 112 or 061

Fire Department: 112 or 080 (local Firefighters)

Country Code Spain: +34

British representations abroad in Spain

Website: https://www.gov.uk/world/organisations/british-embassy-madrid

Embassy of the United Kingdom

Torre Espacio
Paseo de la Castellana, 259 D
28046 Madrid
+34 917 146 300
https://www.gov.uk/world/organisations/british-embassy-madrid

British Consulates in Spain
British Consulate Alicante

Rambla Méndez Núñez, 28-32 - 6º planta
03002 Alicante

+34 965 216 002

British Consulate in Las Palmas de Gran Canaria

Calle Luis Morote, 6 - 3º. Puerto de la Luz
35007 Las Palmas de Gran Canaria
+34 928 262 508

British Consulate in Málaga

Calle Mauricio Moro Pareto, 2
29006 Málaga
+34 952 352 300

British Consulate in Palma de Mallorca

Calle Convent dels Caputxins, n. 4
07002 Palma
+34 971 712 445

British Consulate in Santa Cruz de Tenerife

Plaza Weyler, 8 - 1º
38003 Santa Cruz de Tenerife
+34 928 262 508

British Consulate in Ibiza

Avenida Isidoro Macabich, 45 - 1º 1ª
07800 Ibiza
+34 971 146 300

British Consulate General in Barcelona

Avenida Diagonal, 477 - 13º

08036 Barcelona
+34 917 146 300

US-American representations abroad in Spain

Website: https://es.usembassy.gov/u-s-citizen-services/

Embassy of the United States

Torre Espacio
Paseo de la Castellana, 259 D
28046 Madrid
+34 917 146 300
https://www.gov.uk/world/organisations/british-embassy-madrid

British Consulates in Spain

US Consulate General in Barcelona

Paseo Reina Elisenda de Montcada, 23
08034 Barcelona
+34 93 280 22 27

US Consular Agency Málaga

Avenida Juan Gómez "Juanito", 8
Edificio Lucía 1º-C
29640 Fuengirola (Málaga)
+34 952 47 4891

US Consular Agency Seville

Plaza Nueva, 8-B
2ª planta, Oficina E-2
41001 Sevilla
+34 954 218 751

US Consular Agency in Palma de Mallorca

C/ Porto Pi, 8, 9º- D
07015 Palma de Mallorca
+34 971 403 707

US Citizen Service Valencia

C/ Dr. Romagosa, 1
2ª planta, puerta J
46002 Valencia
+34 963 516 973

US Citizen Service Valencia

Edificio ARCA
C/ Los Martínez Escobar, 3, Oficina 7
35007 Las Palmas
+34 928 27 1259

The Spanish Embassy in the United Kingdom

Embassy of Spain in Reino Unido

39 Chesham Place
London SW1X8SB
+44 020 7235 55 55
http://www.exteriores.gob.es/embajadas/londres/en/pages/
inicio.aspx

The Spanish Embassy in the United States

Embassy of Spain in the United States

2375 Pennsylvania Ave. NW
20037 Washington, D.C.
+1 202 452 0100
http://www.exteriores.gob.es/Embajadas/WASHINGTON/e
n/Embajada/Pages/inicio.aspx

ABOUT THE AUTHOR

Vicki Franz was born in 1993 in Goslar, Germany, and grew up there on the edge of the Harz mountains. After several stays abroad in Asia, the studied tourism manager moved to Barcelona, where she has lived together with her Spanish husband Eduardo since 2016. In 2017, the popular travel blog Vickiviaja.com was born, where today several thousand readers follow Vicki's travel and expat tips. When she's not traveling somewhere far away or in her adopted home of Spain, Vicki is most likely to be found on the beach, in the kitchen, or despairing over the inscrutable Catalan grammar rules.

¡MUCHAS GRACIAS!

A thousand times thank you to everyone who supported me in writing this book: Eduardo for this beautiful book cover and all the encouragement, Zihan for your ideas and support, Silvia for our weekly phone calls and the most beautiful wrists in the world, Melissa, Laura, Maiky, and Jackie as well as my family for various decision support and tips.

Thank you to my expat interview partners and everyone who participated in my expat surveys. I would also like to thank my test readers who contributed some helpful tips and ideas.

If you enjoyed the book, I would be absolutely grateful if you could take a moment to rate it on Amazon.

Further Links and reading

You can find all links in the digital overview on:
https://successfully-moving-to-spain.com/links/or:
https://bit.ly/3KDdgFa or by scanning the following
QR-code with the password: **PAELLA**

[1] https://vickiviaja.com/de/auswandern-ja-oder-nein/
[2] https://www.wetter.de/klima/europa/spanien-c34.html

[3] https://www.currentresults.com/Weather/US/average-annual-precipitation-by-city.php
[4]
https://de.statista.com/statistik/daten/studie/160142/umfr age/arbeitslosenquote-in-den-eu-laendern/#:~:text=Im%20September%202020%20verzeich nete%20Spanien,eine%20der%20h%C3%B6chsten%20Arbei tslosenquoten%20weltweit
[5] https://www.statista.com/statistics/273909/seasonally-adjusted-monthly-unemployment-rate-in-the-us/
[6]
https://www.ons.gov.uk/employmentandlabourmarket/peo pleinwork/employmentandemployeetypes/bulletins/employ mentintheuk/february2023
[7] https://www.worlddata.info/average-income.php
[8] https://happiness-report.s3.amazonaws.com/2022/WHR+22.pdf

[9] https://www.transparency.de/cpi/cpi-2022/cpi-2022-tabellarische-rangliste

[10] https://www.cable.co.uk/broadband/speed/worldwide-speed-league/

[11] https://www.numbeo.com/cost-of-living/country_result.jsp?country=United+States&displayCurrency=EUR

[12] https://www.expatistan.com/cost-of-living/country/united-states

[13] https://www.coinc.es/blog/noticia/ciudad-mas-barata-espana-vivir

[14] https://bit.ly/3mthYwG

[15] https://vickiviaja.com/where-should-i-live-in-spain-quiz/

[16] https://pathforeurope.eu/the-battle-for-the-jus-soli/

[17] https://xyuandbeyond.com/how-to-get-an-eu-passport-citizenship-by-descent/

[18] https://www.sepe.es/HomeSepe/en/empresas/informacion-para-empresas/profesiones-de-dificil-cobertura/profesiones-mas-demandadas

[19] http://www.exteriores.gob.es/Consulados/LOSANGELES/en/InformacionParaExtranjeros/Documents/Checklist%20Work%20Employment%20Visa.pdf

[20] http://www.exteriores.gob.es/Consulados/LOSANGELES/es/InformacionParaExtranjeros/Documents/Copia%20de%20Tabla%20medios%20econ%C3%B3micos%20a%C3%B1o%202017.pdf

[21] http://www.exteriores.gob.es/Consulados/LOSANGELES/en/InformacionParaExtranjeros/Documents/Checklist%20Work%20Employment%20Visa.pdf

[22] http://www.exteriores.gob.es/Consulados/LOSANGELES/en/InformacionParaExtranjeros/Pages/Study-Visa-for-more-than-180-days.aspx

23 https://www.immigrationspain.es/en/civil-partnership/
24 https://administracion.gob.es/pag_Home/en/Tu-espacio-europeo/derechos-obligaciones/ciudadanos/residencia/obtencion-residencia/inscribir-familiares-no-ue.html#:~:text=Family%20members%20must%20apply%20for,at%20the%20relevant%20local%20police
25 https://extranjeros.inclusion.gob.es/ficheros/InformacionInteres/folletos_informativos/archivos/triptico_reagrupacion_familiar_eng.pdf
26 https://immigration-portal.ec.europa.eu/index_en
27 https://ec.europa.eu/immigration/blue-card/spain_en
28 https://ec.europa.eu/immigration/blue-card/essential-information_en
29 https://www.immigrationspain.es/en/visa-for-digital-nomads/
30 https://extranjeros.inclusion.gob.es/UnidadGrandesEmpresas/ficheros/solicitudes/MI_T.pdf
31 http://www.exteriores.gob.es/consulados/washington/en/consulado/pages/visas.aspx
32 https://www.ssa.gov/international/Agreement_Pamphlets/documents/Spain.pdf
33 https://www.gov.uk/government/publications/spain-tax-treaties
34 https://ec.europa.eu/social/main.jsp?catId=1129&intPageId=4795&langId=de
35 https://administracion.gob.es/pag_Home/en/Tu-espacio-europeo/derechos-obligaciones/ciudadanos/trabajo-jubilacion/reconocimiento-cualificaciones/asistencia.html
36 http://www.educacionyfp.gob.es/dam/jcr:9f4ff1e0-d090-4fb9-8be9-270d4442cded/181029-solicitud-equivalencia.pdf
37 https://universidades.sede.gob.es/procedimientos/portada/ida/3513/idp/1029

38
https://www.educacion.gob.es/aefpc/servlet/verdocumento
39 http://www.educacionyfp.gob.es/servicios-al-
ciudadano/catalogo/gestion-titulos/estudios-no-
universitarios/titulos-extranjeros/homologacion-
convalidacion-no-universitarios.html
40 https://taxsummaries.pwc.com/spain/individual/foreign-
tax-relief-and-tax-treaties
41 https://www.bankinter.com/blog/finanzas-
personales/como-calcular-retenciones-irpf-nomina
42
https://sede.agenciatributaria.gob.es/Sede/procedimientoin
i/GI34.shtml
43 https://www.irs.gov/businesses/international-
businesses/spain-tax-treaty-documents
44
https://sede.agenciatributaria.gob.es/Sede/procedimientoin
i/GF00.shtml
45
https://sede.agenciatributaria.gob.es/Sede/procedimientoin
i/G606.shtml
46https://ec.europa.eu/social/main.jsp?catId=1129&intPageI
d=4790&langId=de
47 https://www.aphis.usda.gov/aphis/pet-travel/by-
country/eu/pettravel-spain
48 https://www.mapa.gob.es/en/ganaderia/temas/comercio-
exterior-ganadero/anexoiirue577_2013_tcm38-104902.pdf
49 https://www.mapa.gob.es/en/ganaderia/temas/comercio-
exterior-
ganadero/2013_0577_anexoiv_es_declaracion_tcm30-
104903bilingueesen_01_11_2019_tcm38-512665.docx
50 https://www.aphis.usda.gov/aphis/pet-travel/by-
country/eu/pettravel-spain
51 https://www.mapa.gob.es/en/ganaderia/temas/comercio-
exterior-ganadero/listapuntosentrada03122021_tcm38-
537940.pdf
52 https://www.mapa.gob.es/en/ganaderia/temas/comercio-
exterior-ganadero/desplazamiento-animales-
compania/dogs-cats-ferrets.aspx

53
https://www.exteriores.gob.es/DocumentosAuxiliaresSC/Es
tados%20Unidos/CHICAGO%20%28C%29/tasas.pdf
54
http://www.exteriores.gob.es/Consulados/LONDRES/en/C
onsulado/Documents/Fee%20list%20British%20citizens.pd
f
55
http://www.exteriores.gob.es/Consulados/TORONTO/en/S
erviciosConsulares/Pages/Fees($-CAD).aspx
56 https://www.iprem.com.es/2022.html
57 https://www.edo.cjis.gov/#/
58 https://www.acro.police.uk/Police-Certificates-Online
59 https://travel.state.gov/content/travel/en/records-and-
authentications/authenticate-your-document/apostille-
requirements.html
60 https://www.gov.uk/get-document-legalised
61
http://www.exteriores.gob.es/Consulados/LOSANGELES/e
s/InformacionParaExtranjeros/Documents/English%20Che
cklist%20Self%20Employ%20Work.pdf
62
http://www.exteriores.gob.es/Consulados/LOSANGELES/e
s/InformacionParaExtranjeros/Documents/EX07-
Formulario_cta_propia_imprimible.pdf
63
http://www.exteriores.gob.es/Consulados/LOSANGELES/e
s/InformacionParaExtranjeros/Documents/Modelo%20790
%20c%c3%b3digo%20052%20TASAS.pdf +
http://www.exteriores.gob.es/Consulados/LOSANGELES/e
s/InformacionParaExtranjeros/Documents/InfoM790C52.p
df
64
https://sede.administracionespublicas.gob.es/pagina/index/
directorio/tasa062
65 https://uptapv.org/extranjeria/
66 https://www.gov.uk/find-local-council
67 https://www.gov.uk/government/publications/income-
tax-leaving-the-uk-getting-your-tax-right-p85

68

https://sede.policia.gob.es/portalCiudadano/extranjeria/EX15.pdf

69

https://sede.policia.gob.es/portalCiudadano/extranjeria/EX15.pdf

70

https://sede.policia.gob.es/Tasa790_012/ImpresoRellenar

71

https://play.google.com/store/apps/details?id=com.citaextranjeria.extranjeria

72

https://sede.administracionespublicas.gob.es/icpplus/index.html

73

https://play.google.com/store/apps/details?id=com.citaextranjeria.extranjeria

74

https://play.google.com/store/apps/details?id=com.citaextranjeria.extranjeria

75

https://sede.administracionespublicas.gob.es/icpplus/index.html

76

https://play.google.com/store/apps/details?id=com.citaextranjeria.extranjeria

77

https://seuelectronica.ajuntament.barcelona.cat/APPS/portaltramits/formulari/ptbaltapadro/T06a/init/es/PTCIU.html?

78

https://gestionturnos.madrid.es/GNSIS_WBCIUDADANO/tramite.do

79

https://extranjeros.inclusion.gob.es/ficheros/Modelos_solicitudes/mod_solicitudes2/17-Formulario_TIE.pdf

80

https://extranjeros.inclusion.gob.es/ficheros/modelos_solicitudes/ley_14_2013/MI_TIE_NOV_2018.pdf

81
https://sede.policia.gob.es:38089/Tasa790_012/ImpresoRe
llenar
82
https://sede.administracionespublicas.gob.es/icpplus/index.
html
83
https://play.google.com/store/apps/details?id=com.citaextr
anjeria.extranjeria
84 https://www.mmmm.es/de/blogs-lawyers/spanien-
immobilienrecht/spanisches-mietrecht/)
85 https://www.gov.uk/guidance/how-to-buy-property-in-
spain

86 https://howtobuyinspain.com/en/real-cost-owning-
spanish-property/

87 https://www.sepe.es/HomeSepe
88 https://www.sepe.es/HomeSepe/Personas/distributiva-
prestaciones/Cuantias-anuales.html
89 https://www.infoautonomos.com/seguridad-social/cuota-
de-autonomos-cuanto-se-
paga/#:~:text=Cuota%20de%20aut%C3%B3nomos%20en%
202020,-
90 https://balcellsgroup.com/how-to-become-autonomo-in-
spain/

91
https://www.agenciatributaria.gob.es/AEAT.sede/tramitaci
on/G322.shtml
92 https://www.international-schools-
database.com/country/spain
93
https://de.statista.com/statistik/daten/studie/73631/umfra
ge/durchschnittliches-alter-beim-auszug-aus-dem-
elternhaus/
94 https://unedasiss.uned.es/home&idioma=en
95
http://www.studyinspain.info/en/reportajes/propuestas/Ho
w-to-obtain-a-grant-to-study-in-Spain/

96
https://extranjeros.inclusion.gob.es/ficheros/Modelos_solic
itudes/mod_solicitudes2/18-
Certificado_residencia_comunitaria.pdf
97
https://sede.policia.gob.es/Tasa790_012/ImpresoRellenar
98
https://sede.administracionespublicas.gob.es/icpplus/index.
html
99
https://play.google.com/store/apps/details?id=com.citaextr
anjeria.extranjeria
100 https://itv.com.es/como-matricular-coche-extranjero

101 https://itv.com.es/cita-previa
102 https://sede.dgt.gob.es/es/permisos-de-conducir/canje-
permisos/paises-convenio-bilateral/index.shtml
103
https://sedeclave.dgt.gob.es/WEB_NCIT_CONSULTA/solic
itarCita.faces
104 https://sede.dgt.gob.es/es/permisos-de-
conducir/obtencion-renovacion-duplicados-
permiso/permiso-conducir/index.shtml
105 https://vickiviaja.com/living-abroad-in-spain/
106 https://www.irs.gov/individuals/international-
taxpayers/foreign-earned-income-exclusion-bona-fide-
residence-test
107 https://www.irs.gov/individuals/international-
taxpayers/foreign-earned-income-exclusion

Printed in Great Britain
by Amazon

20274297R00119